"*Lectio divina*, recently promoted by Pope Benedict, is at the center of this author's life. He practices it and has promoted it by his writings and conferences for over twenty-five years. His *St. Joseph Guide to Lectio Divina* shows how *lectio divina* is helpful for the delicate, at times volatile, gender relationships by using the model of the Holy Family. Mary and Joseph lived with the Incarnate Word of God; they can, therefore, help today's women and men to relate to the Word of God. Mary and Joseph exemplify gender mutuality and spiritual integration, each of them in a different way. Mary reveals the dignity and possibilities of femininity by *receiving* the Word while Joseph teaches us about masculinity by *responding* to the Word."

—Walter Vogels, M.Afr., Professor emeritus
Bible Faculty of Theology, Saint Paul University, Ottawa

"Karl Schultz's work highlights a valuable tradition in the Church, *lectio divina*, which is the call to all of us to deeper reflection on the words of Sacred Scripture and, ultimately, greater holiness of life. In this "School of the Word," the author provides a scriptural call to discernment, decision, and action. All who enter into this practice will find a real spiritual treasure."

—Bishop David A. Zubik, Diocese of Pittsburgh

"Karl A. Schultz offers wonderful insights on the ways that Mary and Joseph can be mentors for *lectio divina*. Their receptivity to God's word, their marital relationship, and their balance of the contemplative and active dimensions help us understand the holistic and creative elements within the ancient art of *lectio divina*."

—Stephen J. Binz
Author of *Conversing with God in Scripture:
A Contemporary Approach to Lectio Divina*

"*Lectio divina* has been too long ignored, even though this is a method of experiencing God that has been a time-honored way of prayer for those seeking a deep level of contemplative connection with God. Now, Karl Schultz has presented a re-discovery of *lectio divina*, showing how this historical form of prayer, where one seeks and reaches that core place of 'resting in God,' can be reached. At this level we then surprisingly discover the crucial bearing the word of God has on our lives, and on our world.

"The author's *St. Joseph Guide to Lectio Divina* brings us to see that the central truth of our lives is that God passionately desires our union with Him, and that if we actually engage with God's love, a power results that can make this world the 'garden of paradise' it was meant to be. If ever a book on this theme were needed, there couldn't be a more 'needy' time than the present!"

—Antoinette Bosco
Author of *Radical Forgiveness*

"In his latest book, Karl Schultz offers not only a personal and creative exploration of *lectio divina* but pays welcome tribute to Cardinal Carlo Martini, S.J., a pioneer in the revival of *lectio divina* in our time."

—George Martin
Founding editor, *God's Word Today*

"People want to find a way to pray—and many are tired of following the latest trends. Karl Schultz presents the method of the saints in a way that's fresh and even startling. Where better to learn the ways of prayer than in the company of the Holy Family? Put this book to work. It'll transform your life."

—Mike Aquilina, Executive Vice President
St. Paul Center for Biblical Theology

"Karl Schultz continues to be a premier exponent of the joy and spiritual growth that comes from sacred reading, *lectio divina*. Fresh from his three month tour in Australia and New Zealand where he lectured successfully on *lectio*, Schultz has a slam-dunk in this excellent *St. Joseph Guide to Lectio Divina*. What makes his contribution so unique is its invitation to join our Blessed Lady and St. Joseph, the Holy Family, using *lectio*, to grow in age, grace, and wisdom before the Lord and others. We can see why Pope Benedict XVI, generously quoted by Schultz, has put such an emphasis on *lectio* as a spiritual instrument for our times."

—Fr. Timothy Fitzgerald, C.P., STD
St. Paul of the Cross Retreat Center, Pittsburgh, PA

*St. Joseph*

# Guide to
# *Lectio Divina*

*Sharing the Word with
the Holy Family*

**Karl A. Schultz**

CATHOLIC BOOK PUBLISHING CORP.
New Jersey

NIHIL OBSTAT: Rev. Donald E. Blumenfeld, Ph.D.
       *Censor Librorum*

IMPRIMATUR: ✛ Most Rev. John J. Myers, J.C.D., D.D.
       *Archbishop of Newark*

"The Ancient Art of *Lectio Divina*" reprinted here with the permission of Luke Dysinger, O.S.B.

"The School of the Word" translated by Matthew J. O'Connell, *Worship* (Vol. 61, 5), May 1987, and reproduced here with the permission of the publishers.

Cover image: Anton Raphael Mengs, German, 1728-1779
*The Dream of Joseph*, c. 1773
Oil on wood panel, 43³/₄ x 34 inches, SN328
Bequest of John Ringling, 1936, collection of The John and Mable Ringling Museum of Art, the State Art Museum of Florida, a division of Florida State University.

(T-657)

ISBN 978-0-89942-677-8

Printed in U.S.A.
www.catholicbookpublishing.com

# Table of Contents

# DEDICATION

*To Mom and Dad,*
*Loving and Missing You Always, Karl*

# PRAYER

Mary and Joseph, pray for us always, and help us to follow your example in fidelity to your Son, the Word, Jesus.

St. Joseph, continue to teach me what it means to be a just and merciful man.

Mary, help us find peace, joy, and love by uniting our hurts and wounds with yours in union with your Son, Jesus.

# ACKNOWLEDGMENTS

Thanks and love to Marc and Brian for being wonderful brothers.

Remembering and loving Uncle Tom, Big T, for his love, humility, humor, and caring presence. Yerrrrrrr.

I would like to thank Fr. Tim Fitzgerald, CP, for his friendship, guidance, understanding, and support.

Thanks to Rachel, my caring cousin with whom I have shared much of the journey.

I am grateful for the navigational assistance, counsel, and friendship of the Commodore, Neal Murphy. As we've often observed, there is no smooth sailing in rough waters.

I appreciate the support of my editor, Emilie Cerar. Em allowed me to write the book the best way I know how, and to address essential issues from the heart and mind in union with the Holy Family and the Church.

# Introduction

## The "Edict" of Benedict:
## The Papal Charter for *Lectio Divina*

" . . . I WOULD like in particular to recall and recommend the ancient tradition of *Lectio divina*. . . . If it is effectively promoted, this practice will bring to the Church—I am convinced of it—a new spiritual springtime. As a strong point of biblical ministry, *Lectio divina* should therefore be increasingly encouraged, also through the use of new methods, carefully taught through and in step with the times" (Benedict XVI, address to the Catholic Biblical Federation, September 16, 2005).

I playfully and wistfully refer to Pope Benedict's seminal statement on *lectio divina* as an edict because I wish it was taken as such. It is a profound and eloquent exhortation for several reasons:

First, it articulates succinctly in potent language that traditional and modern wisdom should be integrated in the practice of *lectio divina*. This belies media characterizations of Benedict as regressive and reactionary. I am exceedingly grateful for this papal mandate to prudently utilize cutting edge, credible, and orthodox concepts and methods in service of the faithful. Pope Benedict is exhorting us to be:

- prudent / responsible ("carefully thought through");
- progressive, innovative ("new methods");
- pastoral ("in step with the times");
- enthusiastic ("increasingly encouraged").

Second, in line with Church documents emphasizing proper use of modern communication technologies and organizational and developmental practices, it encourages effective promotion and instruction. We must use our human resources and opportunities wisely in service of the divine word. The "business" or administrative end of catechetics, pastoral ministry, and evangelization is often overlooked. I received a degree in Accounting from the Ross School of Business Administration at the University of Michigan, so I have an appreciation of this dimension of Christian service. All of our human talents and experiences have utility in our vocation.

Here the pope is converging practicality, pedagogy, and pastoral care. Since its inception, the Church has usually sought to use the technologies and resources at her disposal in order to disseminate the Gospel. Reactionary measures against progress in response to abuses and threats inevitably become counterproductive.

The Church, and each person, function best when they pursue constructive remedies to dilemmas rather than sulk in defensive postures. Vatican II was a departure from the siege mentality that ensued in response to the Reformation. In accordance with Benedict's vision, through the individual and collective practice of *lectio divina* the Council's fruits can be realized in our lives.

The pope uses a term that is becoming increasingly common in the Catholic vernacular: biblical ministry. We take up this challenge in this book by moving beyond standard *lectio divina* fare. We address applications such as dialogue, potential fulfillment, and gender identity and relations that are rarely dealt with because they require competence in fields beyond that of biblical studies, spirituality, and theology that have a subjective and potentially controversial dimension. *Lectio divina* is simple and straightforward enough for its essence to be explained succinctly. However, to progress in the practice, to share, teach, and persevere with it in the face of significant interior and external obstacles requires a more advanced, refined approach that thankfully is within the competence even of absolute beginners. You'll discover this as you become familiar with *lectio* and work through this book.

## The Biblical Renewal

Pope Benedict has carefully read the signs of the times and recognizes that a biblical renewal is long overdue in the Church. As a professional theologian he is rightfully critical of irresponsible scholarship and academic abstractions that distort Church teaching and the formation of the faithful. His weekly audiences and writings are great material for *lectio divina*. Like Cardinal Martini, he has an uncommon knack for humanizing Scripture, offering penetrating expositions, and making complex topics accessible and practical. He called the Synod and composed an apostolic exhortation on the Bible. He is supportive of the efforts of the Catholic Biblical Federation, and frequently promotes *lectio* and other forms of biblical spirituality and ministry such as Bible-sharing groups, family prayer, and adult religious education.

## Who This Book Is For

This book is for persons at all levels of familiarity with Scripture, *lectio divina*, and the Holy Family. While introductory, it also includes intermediate and advanced concepts and practices in accessible language.

There is a huge void in Christian publishing with respect to post-introductory, non-technical, "more than" materials. There is an abundance of resources for beginners, but little for the non-scholar who is seeking more. This book reflects my confidence in your ability to assimilate and apply stimulating material.

## Book Structure

Chapter one is a detailed overview and explanation of *lectio divina*.

Chapter two moves into the biblical ministry realm by considering familial, pastoral, and cultural contexts which influence and potentially impede the practice of *lectio divina*. In short, it discusses how to practice *lectio* on the run. Just as travelers learn how to survive on a budget, so we can discover how to thrive spiritually under time, energy, and financial constraints. Two of my books may also be helpful in this quest: *Personal Energy Management: A Christian Personal and Professional Growth Program* and *Calming the Stormy Seas of Stress.*

Chapter three deals with the fundamental theological and anthropological characteristics of God's word and the accompanying human and divine signs by which it is manifested and discerned in contemporary life. It explores the sacramental essence and various manifestations of the word of God in anticipation of a discussion of a *lectio*-based model for confession in chapter four.

Chapter four deals with dialogue, the fundamental mode and dynamic of *lectio divina.*

Chapter five addresses contemporary gender issues in relation to *lectio divina* and the model of Mary and Joseph. *Lectio divina* is an ideal tool for addressing gender issues because it is holistic, balanced, and proactive rather than reactive. It is critical (getting to the essence of things) and open rather than judgmental, moralistic, or prejudicial. It focuses on listening to and receiving from God and others in conjunction with our own input. It enables us to read and respond to the signs of the times and our lives in an inspired, loving, and truthful manner. The Bible provides many gender-related narratives and counsels as source material for *lectio.* The greatest models are Mary and Joseph, whom we discuss from a counter-cultural, vocational, and developmental perspective in chapters six and seven.

Chapter six focuses on Mary as a model of discipleship and a feminine approach to Scripture and *lectio divina,* a subject equally appropriate for men. It surveys Marian biblical texts and offers contemporary applications and reflection questions. It begins and ends with a poignant biblical synthesis by Pope Paul VI.

Chapter seven concludes the book with its namesake, St. Joseph, the silent saint particularly beloved by women. He says little or nothing, mercifully and patiently extends the benefit of the doubt to family members (a virtue expounded upon eloquently by St. Francis de Sales in his *Introduction to the Devout Life*), heeds divine directives, stays in the background, and enables his wife to receive appropriate attention and praise (cf. Prov 31:10-31), protects and provides for the family, and is a chaste and faithful husband and a dutiful father. Joseph is the model par excellence for men, husbands, and fathers, and his example of discipleship is second only to Mary's. In light of his low profile and the contemporary need for a wholesome and holy model of masculinity, we can justly state that we have saved the best for last!

## Mary and Joseph, Models of Gender and Spiritual Complementarity

Mary and Joseph exemplify gender mutuality and spiritual integration. Joseph obeys the word in deed, while Mary reflects deeply on it and consents completely. She also dares to ask questions of God, whether through the Angel or in the person of Jesus. Her example encourages us to be candid with God and, as St. Thérèse Lisieux emphasized, confident in His goodwill towards us.

Neither Mary nor Joseph could or tried to carry out the other's vocation. There is no contentiousness or competition. An excellent book on the dynamics of the Holy Family is Fr. Lucien Deiss' *Joseph, Mary, Jesus*. Fr. Deiss was a significant contributor to the biblical and liturgical renewal that followed Vatican II.

Mary models femininity and Joseph masculinity. Recently, there has been a grassroots movement within American Catholicism, in emulation of Evangelical Protestantism, to identify masculinity with the myths of warrior and wild-man while emphasizing basic devotions. While there are elements of truth in these metaphors, we have a superior and inspired model in Joseph. The final chapter of the book explores the truth about masculinity as revealed in Joseph. This is desperately needed today as an antidote to absent and false father images.

Much of the mass carnage in the twentieth century can be directly traced to false images and demonstrations of masculinity manifested by dictatorial leaders. Abortion, a parallel false metaphor for women's liberation, has produced a silent, but no less grievous carnage. An excellent book on the decline and misdirection of paternal influence, and its exacerbation in the post-industrial age, is Jungian analyst Luigi Zoja's *The Father: Historical, Psychological and Cultural Perspectives.*

Joseph is the universal patron of the Church. The term guardian fits him well. He oversees, protects, and defends. He is an advocate for both sexes, and a valuable resource for unity.

Mary is the mother of the Church. She is the ultimate life-giver and nurturer. At the cross her vocation as mother of sorrows and the Church emerged. Within the Catholic tradition there are numerous inspiring reflections (including most recently, works of Archbishop Sheen and Cardinal Martini, e.g., *Our Lady of Holy Saturday*) that highlight the hope nurtured by the mother of God as she awaited the resurrection. Towards the end of her life, Mary experienced suffering in its most insidious form, the loss of her husband and the shameful crucifixion of her Son, but allowed God to redeem and infuse her suffering with divine love and wisdom.

Conversely, at the beginning of his adult life, Joseph experienced one of the greatest wounds one can sustain, that of apparent spousal infidelity. With no tidy resolution, he sought to balance justice and mercy and put the interests of his betrothed above his own. Joseph is a real man in every sense of the expression, just as Mary is, in Jesus' own words, Woman.

The gender dimension of our interactions with God's word and the fulfillment of our potential are overlooked areas in theological, anthropological, and sociological studies. Not any more. With the two finest human models at our disposal, we will use the unparalleled developmental model of *lectio divina* to reflect on how together we can join Mary and Joseph in hearing the word of God and carrying it out.

## Biblical References

Biblical references use the standard nomenclature that is explained in most Bibles and in my previous books, *The St. Joseph Guide to the Bible*, *The How-To Book of the Bible*, and *How to Pray with the Bible*.

In brief, the abbreviation of a biblical book is followed by the chapter number, then a colon to designate verses. A range of chapters or verses is indicated by a hyphen, and a selection of non-consecutive chapters or verses by a comma. A semi-colon designates different biblical books or references.

Cf. stands for cross-reference, and is used when referring to one or more passages, but not quoting them. When quoting a passage, no cross-reference indicator is necessary.

For example, Gen 1:2-3 stands for chapter one of Genesis, verses two through three.

Exod 4:1, 14 indicates the first and fourteenth verses of the fourth chapter of Exodus.

Ps 14:2; 15:3 implies the second verse of the fourteenth psalm and the third verse of the fifteenth psalm.

Two of the most helpful aids in Bibles are the cross-references and footnotes. The cross-references identify related passages and let the Bible interpret itself by exposing its larger context and cohesive meaning. Footnotes explain difficult passages and ambiguities in the original language or manuscript tradition.

## The Appendix

The Appendix contains articles on *lectio divina* from two leading proponents, Cardinal Carlo M. Martini, S.J., and Fr. Luke Dysinger, O.S.B. Consistent with my emphasis on the diverse and flexible nature of *lectio divina*, these bring out different aspects of the practice according to the author's religious charism and expertise. I include alternative perspectives in the appendices of my books because I want to expose the reader to the diverse intellectual and spiritual riches of the Church and the different emphases and proficiencies of my peers.

## Contacting the Author

The dialogical spirit of the book necessitates interaction between author and reader. I welcome feedback, suggestions, and sharing. You can contact me at karlaschultz@juno.com or mrkarleno@gmail.com or by calling (412) 766-7545.

Additional books and audio-video resources by the author are listed in the bibliography in the back of the book and in my website, karlaschultz.com, which also contains information on media, retreat, and public-speaking engagements.

# "NAZARETH, SCHOOL OF THE GOSPEL"

## Tribute of Pope Paul VI to the Mother of God, and Our Mother, the Virgin Mary

"NAZARETH is the school in which we begin to understand the life of Jesus. It is the school of the Gospel. Here we learn to observe, to listen, to meditate, and to penetrate the profound and mysterious meaning of that simple, humble, and lovely manifestation of the Son of God. And perhaps we learn almost imperceptibly to imitate Him. Here we learn the method by which we can come to understand Christ. Here we discover the need to observe the milieu of His sojourn among us—places, period of time, customs, language, religious practices, all of which Jesus used to reveal Himself to the world. Here everything speaks to us; everything has meaning.

". . . The lesson of silence: may there return to us an appreciation of this stupendous and indispensable spiritual condition, deafened as we are by so much tumult, so much noise, so many voices of our chaotic and frenzied modern life. O silence of Nazareth, teach us recollection, reflection, and eagerness to heed the good inspirations and words of true teachers; teach us the need and value of preparation, of study, of meditation, of interior life, of secret prayer seen by God alone.

"The lesson of domestic life: may Nazareth teach us the meaning of family life, its harmony of love, its simplicity and austere beauty, its sacred and inviolable character; may it teach us how sweet and irreplaceable is its training, how fundamental and incomparable its role on the social plane.

"The lesson of work: O Nazareth, home of 'the carpenter's son,' we want here to understand and to praise the austere and redeeming law of human labor, here to restore the consciousness of the dignity of labor, here to recall that work cannot be an end in itself, and that it is free and ennobling in proportion to the values—beyond the economic ones—which motivate it.

We would like here to salute all the workers of the world, and to point out to them their great Model, their Divine Brother, the Champion of all their rights, Christ the Lord!

". . . Christ in His Gospel has spelled out for the world the supreme purpose and the noblest force for action and hence for liberty and progress: love. No goal can surpass it, be superior to it, or supplant it. The only sound law of life is His Gospel. The human person reaches his highest level in Christ's teaching. Human society finds therein its most genuine and powerful unifying force.

"We believe, O Lord, in Thy word; we will try to follow and live it.

". . . Now we hear its echo reverberating in the souls of men of our century. It seems to tell us: Blessed are we, if in poverty of spirit we learn to free ourselves from false confidence in material things and to place our chief desires in spiritual and religious goods, treating the poor with respect and love as brothers and living images of Christ.

"Blessed are we, if, having acquired the meekness of the strong, we learn to renounce the deadly power of hate and vengeance, and have the wisdom to exalt above the fear of armed force the generosity of forgiveness, alliance in freedom and work, and conquest through goodness and peace.

"Blessed are we, if we do not make egoism the guiding criterion of our life, nor pleasure its purpose, but learn rather to discover in sobriety our strength, in pain a source of redemption, in sacrifice the very summit of greatness.

"Blessed are we, if we prefer to be the oppressed rather than the oppressors, and constantly hunger for the progress of justice.

"Blessed are we, if for the Kingdom of God in time and beyond time we learn to pardon and to persevere, to work and to serve, to suffer and to love.

"We shall never be deceived.

"In such accents do we seem to hear His voice today. Then, it was stronger, sweeter, and more awe-inspiring: it was divine.

But as we try to recapture some echo of the Master's words, we seem to be won over as His disciples and to be genuinely filled with new wisdom and fresh courage."

*—Pope Paul VI address*
*at the Basilica of the Annunciation*
*in Nazareth, January 5, 1964*

# – One –

## Reading the Bible Prayerfully and Holistically
## The Ancient Art of *Lectio Divina*

"IN the history of Moses, as in the other events recorded in the Bible, we find realities that are repeated in the life of every individual. Anyone who is inwardly open and acquainted with prayer can find in the words of scripture what is needed for his or her life.

"It seems to me that the decisive questions to be asked by each person are:

"What does this scripture passage mean to me? What is it saying to me? How is it related to my life?

"We might at first say, 'It doesn't have anything to do with my life.' But rather than remain with such a first impression, we should look for the cause and ask, 'Why is there no connection between this Bible passage and my life? What would I want the connection to be?' In this way, even a negative first impression can be a means of contact between what the Bible says and what we experience.

"Often this contact does not take place immediately, but only after we have entered into a dialogue, a wrestling with the words of scripture. Only then does it begin to shed light. Such a dialogue is a decisive help toward prayer, which springs from our center and expresses our deepest yearnings. This is the aim of spiritual guidance: To help us express ourselves in prayer as we are, in keeping with our situation and nature. Real prayer is not child's play. Scripture teaches us that prayer is a struggle, a battle. It places us face to face with our greatest difficulties. In prayer we are trained to look at the problems of our life with an open eye and to accept them, for human beings are often afraid to confront themselves."

("*From Moses to Jesus: The Way of the Paschal Mystery,* Carlo M. Martini. S.J.)

The Catholic tradition is home to western civilization's oldest and most natural, universal, and holistic model of potential fulfillment, spiritual communications, and biblical spirituality. You've experienced it in some form and degree, even if you are unaware of the vocabulary or process. It is a seminal, integrated process that persons of all cultures and creeds engage in reflexively as part of the dialogical reading and communication process.

*Lectio* (leks-ee-oh) *divina* (di-veen-a) is the Latin term for divine or sacred reading or listening. Initially it applied primarily to reading or listening to the Bible, whether privately or within the family, clan, or community. It was subsequently applied to the writings of the Church fathers (which are often expositions of the biblical texts). Because of traditional usage and the difficulty of translating it precisely, the Latin expression (often abbreviated to *lectio*) is commonly used.

In biblical times books were rare and expensive, and most folks couldn't read. Because communal listening rather than individual reading was the most common way our ancestors encountered the Bible, it is also accurate to refer to *lectio divina* as *listening* to the Bible, remembering that St. Paul observed that faith comes through hearing (cf. Rom 10:17). The ancients believed that sound came in through the ear and then proceeded funnel-like into the chamber of the heart.

I refer to *lectio divina* in the subtitle of this chapter as an art because unlike a science, it cannot adequately be defined in technical terms, and it has a significant subjective element. It is an art in the sense that our communications with God and others transcend words and can ultimately only be comprehended, however imperfectly, through experience.

## Components of *Lectio Divina*

In the early Church, praying the Scriptures holistically was described in terms of reading and prayer. With the development of the practice under the desert fathers and the monks, reading expanded to include the term meditation, and the receptive side of prayer was distinctly identified as contemplation, which in its original Greek, *theoria*, means seeing. In the Middle Ages, the stage of action was made explicit, though it has always been implied. The following is a brief discussion of each component, which we will elaborate on shortly.

*Reading:* Slowly read a brief portion of Scripture, and if practical, aloud, even in a whisper or murmur, thereby engaging more of the senses.

*Transitional activity, bridging reading to meditation:* Select a word, phrase, sentence, verse, image, or theme that speaks to you. Another way of referring to this is as a "divine sign," that is, a word or stimulus that speaks to you. Human signs of the times or your life can also be venues through which God speaks to you in daily life.

The Sunday or daily lectionary is a great source for *lectio* passages because the various readings: Old Testament, psalm, epistle, and Gospel, affirm, balance, or in some cases contrast with each other to bring out the fullness of God's message. This helps us to read the Bible contextually, rather than in a vacuum.

*Meditation:* Repeat the word, stimulus, or inspiration over and over, gradually internalizing it and enabling it to penetrate the subconscious mind. Such rumination is the most ancient Christian notion of meditation, which was depicted through the image of a cow chewing its cud.

*Optional activity:* In medieval times, monks incorporated the meditative dimensions of both practical application (which has always been implied) and discursive reflection, that is, moving from one thought to another. Medieval monks coined the term *reminiscence* to describe the reflexive linking of the biblical word or passage at hand with other biblical themes or passages or life experiences that come to mind. Just as memories build up in a vocation, profession, or relationship, this happens naturally as we become increasingly exposed to and familiar with Scripture.

However, we should be careful not to habitually lose sight of our original word or inspiration and enter into a diffuse stream of consciousness with regards to Scripture and our time and conversation with God. If we too quickly move on to other passages, we may lack substance in our *lectio* and avoid the meaning of the text before us.

*Prayer:* Share our reactions to our word or the biblical passage with God, offering Him our emotions and response in a conversational manner, whether silently or aloud. When doing *lectio* in a group, we can also share them with others. See *The St. Joseph Guide to the Bible* for a model of group Bible-sharing using the format of *lectio divina.*

*Contemplation:* Listen receptively for God's response in the silence of our hearts. Pay attention to the Spirit's stirring. Don't expect an Angel to whisper in your ear. Recalling the term used by Brother Lawrence in *The Practice of the Presence of God,* contemplation is receptive "simple presence" before the Lord. Just "being" with God, gazing at Him so to speak, sharing the moments as we would with a loved one.

*Action:* Living the word, wrestling with it as we encounter difficulties in understanding and applying it. When we experience the word in action, we often uncover depths of meaning and different perspectives. Using the imagery of an obscure parable of Jesus, God's word is a seed that grows almost imperceptibly, in a manner paralleling the kingdom of God (cf. Mk 4:26-29; incidentally, the only parable in Mark not found in Matthew or Luke).

## *Lectio Divina's* Jewish Roots and Parallels

Like much of Christianity, *lectio divina* has its roots in Judaism. The Jewish people developed the principles and practices underlying *lectio divina* when the biblical material was in its oral stage, and refined them over time. Eventually the reading process assimilated a rabbinical interpretive model entitled *pardes*, an acronym meaning orchard or garden that also stands for the four levels of meaning in Scripture:

- *Peshat*: The simple, straightforward, plain, literal, historical meaning.
- *Remez:* The hinted, "clued," allegorical/symbolic meaning.
- *Derash:* The applied meaning or practical application, such as elaborated in homilies.
- *Sod:* The mystical or infused (given by God) meaning.

This rabbinical model continues to be used today within Judaism, and is similar to Christian models for distinguishing levels of meaning in the Bible.

John Cassian, an early desert father, developed a model similar to *pardes* that became the starting point for medieval exegesis (literal interpretation) of Scripture. His categories were:

- The literal/historical;
- The allegorical or Christological (that is, how passages in the Old Testament in particular refer to Christ in a symbolic, anticipatory, prophetic, sense);
- The moral or anthropological (the reader's meaning, what he or she is compelled to do by Scripture);
- The anagogical (leading) or eschatological (end times): where the Bible leads us (towards God and heaven.)

The last three senses have traditionally been grouped together as the spiritual senses. Both the Pontifical Biblical Commission's 1993 document *On the Interpretation of the Bible in the Church* (II, B) and the *Catechism of the Catholic Church* (115-118) present the above model.

In his medieval classic *Morals on the Book of Job*, Pope St. Gregory the Great organizes his comments according to the historical, allegorical, and moral senses. In his *Summa Theologia*, St. Thomas Aquinas affirms the traditional distinction between the literal and spiritual senses, and divides the latter into the symbolic (allegorical) and moral.

Thus in terms of both methodology and practice, the early Church and later the monastic communities drew upon their

Jewish inheritance and peers in developing principles of biblical spirituality and interpretation.

The Benedictines and Cistercians (Trappists) have been major influences in *lectio divina's* development and dissemination, while the Carmelites, Franciscans, and even a prominent Jesuit, Cardinal Carlo M. Martini, have incorporated their community's spirituality into the model.

There is no one way to practice *lectio divina*. As a spirituality, communications, and developmental model it is practiced uniquely by each person, in accordance with their capacities, needs, circumstances, and the movement of the Holy Spirit.

### *Lectio Divina's* Source Material

When Christians in the early Church period read or heard the New Testament writings, they processed them the same way they had the Old Testament writings. As mentioned, *lectio* was applied pre-eminently to the Bible, but also to the writings of the Church Fathers (e.g., Augustine, Gregory the Great, Am-brose, Jerome). Today its application to life is becoming increasingly prominent. My books on time management, stress management, journaling, suffering, care-giving, infertility, gender relations, and potential fulfillment explore the application of *lectio* to each.

The Eastern Orthodox tradition has a similar practice called the Jesus Prayer. Articulated in the anonymous spiritual classic *Way of a Pilgrim*, it involves repeating the expression "Lord Jesus Christ, have mercy on me."

Section two of part four of the Pontifical Biblical Commission's *The Interpretation of the Bible in the Church* advocates *lectio* for both private and communal reading of Scripture.

### The Role of Repetition

A Jewish proverb states that reading something ninety-nine times is not the same as reading it a hundred times. This is particularly true with respect to the Bible, and in a number of ways:

First, the *lectio divina* process itself includes repetition of the biblical material, i.e., the "word" that speaks to you.

Second, biblical writers repeat key vocabulary and themes as a means of emphasis. This is an interpretive key that can help us discern the literal meaning of the text. Building upon the literal meaning is crucial to an authentic experience of *lectio divina.* Otherwise we will project personal bias and agenda onto the text and thereby obscure the literal meaning and the movement of the Spirit.

Authentic biblical spirituality is a mixture of comprehension (literal interpretation) and reflection (personal applications and projections of our circumstances and perspectives onto the text). As long as we integrate and balance, and do not confuse these, we can feel confident that we will arrive at the meaning God intends for us, even if it takes awhile to manifest itself. If we persevere, we will gradually and peacefully receive the word and blessing God has for us, even if they come under the guise of trials and suffering (cf. Heb 12:5-7).

Third, sometimes the same story is told in several versions, particularly in the Old Testament and the Gospels. These "doublets" usually indicate multiple sources. Also, it reflects their understanding that a particular event or teaching can be considered from several viewpoints.

## The Stages of *Lectio Divina* in Contemporary Terms

Utilizing the Bible's repetitive, affirming, and multiple perspective approach, I will now present the activities and dynamics of *lectio divina* in contemporary terms using alliteration. In the psalms, this technique is known as acrostic. It is designed to be mnemonic, that is, facilitate memorization and retention.

*Lectio divina* consists of activities that typically unfold in stages, though not necessarily sequentially. Not only does each person process the Bible and life experience uniquely, but such changes with the circumstances and the person's development.

Traditionally, *lectio's* stages have been identified as *reading, meditation, prayer, contemplation,* and *action.* The following alliterative parallels serve as a starting and reference point for the discussion of the traditional stages that follow.

- **Retreat (Refresh/Restore/Renew):** Step back from the hustle-bustle. Make time for daily Sabbath moments.

- **Relax:** Come into God's presence and get settled in, as you would with a friend.

- **Release:** Let God free you of unnecessary anxiety and concerns.

- **Read** . . . slowly, aloud, using all the senses, perhaps following the words with your finger to slow down. This naturally heightens your awareness of the grammatical elements of the text, which also communicate meaning. Select a word, phrase, image, or verse(s) from the passage that touches or teaches you. This "word" can serve as your bridge to the day, a centering point to return to amid the day's activities.

- **Rhythm:** Enter into the flow of God's word and Spirit through gentle oscillation (ranging back and forth) between the various activities. Don't cultivate rigid expectations of what the rhythm should feel like, or worry that you don't have it. It comes naturally with practice and grace, and it is unique to each person.

- **Repeat/Recite:** Gently murmur or recite your "word" repeatedly. This ingrains it in your conscious and subconscious mind as an inspired affirmation.

- **Reflect:** Consider what actions or attitudes your "word" is calling you to. What does it mean to you?

- **Reminisce:** Your "word" may trigger memories of other biblical or life *passages*. The Hebrew word "*pesach*" from which comes the word "paschal" (i.e., mystery, lamb) refers to the Passover and means *passage*, which is the essence of Christian life: a journey home. (See *The Art of Passing Over* by Francis Dorff.) *Reminiscence* (the word coined by the medieval monks to describe this practice) helps you connect the various passages, biblical and experiential, in your life. Like reminiscence, passages link things.

- **Re-create:** Use your imagination to envision the biblical scene and character(s). Our objective is to interact with and imaginatively participate in the text holistically, that is, with all our faculties. To use St. Ignatius of Loyola's terminology, "consider the persons" (identify and perhaps dialogue with them).
- **React:** Share your thoughts and feelings with God, others, or your journal.
- **Receive:** Be present to God in silence. Listen. Experience divine consolation.
- **Rest:** Cool down as preparation for resuming your activities. *Lectio divina* is a spiritual exercise that requires both exertion and relaxation.
- **Respond:** Don't just pray; do something. Practice what you have received.
- **Realize:** Enjoy the fruits of your labor. Discover God's initiative in your life. Experience your "word" bearing fruit in your life in various degrees as described in the parable of the sower (cf. Mk 4:2-20).

## *Lectio Divina's* Fluid Nature

*Lectio divina* is an adaptable, flexible model rather than a rigid method. It isn't a mechanical, linear process. It is fluid, personal, and circumstantial. You oscillate between its stages according to your capacities, circumstances, and the movement of the Spirit. We even change our approach to *lectio* as we grow and our circumstances change. *Lectio* is a dynamic rather than static practice.

Because the activities of *lectio divina* overlap and are related, it is artificial to distinguish between them rigidly. *Lectio divina* is a form of prayer, spiritual communications, and development, and therefore it is not amenable to precise description. Everyone experiences it differently. Like intimacy between spouses, terminology cannot adequately capture the experience.

For example, reading and meditation are essentially two aspects of the same activity of taking in and responding to a biblical or life passage. Prayer and contemplation are the active and receptive aspects of dialogue with God. The early Church originally described this process in terms of reading and prayer. Meditation was considered part of reading, and contemplation was part of prayer. As mentioned, the fifth stage, action, initially was assumed. In the Middle Ages, it was articulated as the consummating stage.

The Vatican II document on Scripture, "The Dogmatic Constitution on Divine Revelation," also known as *Dei Verbum* ("The word of God"), does not specifically mention *lectio divina* by name, though it refers to it through the ancient formula "reading and prayer." Consider how far the Church has come in its promotion of *lectio divina* among the laity. At Vatican II, they didn't even use the term. Now, the pope can hardly give an address or publish a document on the Bible without mentioning *lectio divina*, usually in enthusiastic terms.

*Lectio divina* continues to evolve with its environment: Cardinal Martini of Milan has shown how the components of discernment, decision, and consolation, particularly as understood within the Jesuit tradition, are operative in *lectio divina*. I highly recommend his books, which are insightful and stimulating expositions of key biblical texts using the model of *lectio divina*.

A fascinating aspect of Martini's ministry is that prior to becoming archbishop of Milan he was a renowned professor, "text critic" (expert in ancient biblical manuscripts), and administrator (rector of both the Pontifical Biblical Institute and Gregorian University). This brilliant, cultured academic was to become the worldwide leader in the renaissance of *lectio divina* at the grassroots level, and to publish over forty books in multiple languages aimed primarily at non-academics. Most of his academic writings are of a highly technical nature. Very few persons can integrate and communicate academic and popular understandings in so comprehensive and compelling a manner. An article containing Cardinal Martini's 1986 address on *lectio divina* to the U.S. bishops can be found in the appendix of this book.

Publisher and topic permitting, I make it a practice to include in my books, articles written by peers whom I consider to be at the top of the profession. I want to expose you to diverse, first-rate perspectives on *lectio* and illustrate my assertion that there is no one right way to practice it. Take the various perspectives presented and cull from each one what works for you, and be patient with yourself and God while you go through the trial and error process. If something feels natural and comfortable, you should trust it, at least until you discover a better way. Instant results are neither guaranteed nor necessary. God calls us to be faithful, rather than successful.

## How Does *Lectio* Unfold?

There are as many permutations of *lectio* as there are persons and settings. What you do today may be different from tomorrow. For example, you might begin by reading and then be led by the Spirit to the silence of contemplation. Or perhaps you'll begin by praying your feelings and then move to meditation on your current situation in light of the biblical passage you are reading or reminded of (reminiscence). You might also begin and linger in the silence of contemplation, soaking up God's presence. When you're weary, just being with a loved one is what you need most.

The key is to follow where your faculties and the prompting of the Spirit take you, while eventually incorporating each of the stages. You thereby balance spontaneity and self-discipline, and avoid being too rigid or scrupulous or too lax. Catholicism is a religion of balance, integration, and moderation, attributes that characterize the Bible and human development as well.

## *Lectio* Lesson

Without being scrupulous or mechanical, it is important to incorporate some degree of each of the *lectio* activities at some point in a given session. (This usually happens naturally, so we need not be hyper-conscious of it.) Otherwise our experience may be unbalanced, and even counterproductive, for example:

- If we don't pray, we don't share ourselves with God.
- If we don't engage in contemplation, and thereby listen and rest in God's presence, we won't open ourselves fully to His guidance.
- If we don't read, we lose touch with the inspired source material and fundamental activity, reading. We are unable to inform our prayer with the "word" from the text. Of course, prayer can exist independent of reading, but the advantage of reading is that it gives us divinely inspired substance for our reflections.
- If we don't meditate, the word we received in the reading stage won't take root in us.
- If we don't act on the word, it is lifeless.

An influential medieval proponent of *lectio*, the twelfth century Carthusian monk Guigo II, offers the following helpful synthesis:

" . . . reading without meditation is sterile, meditation without reading is liable to error, prayer without meditation is lukewarm, meditation without prayer is unfruitful, prayer when it is fervent wins contemplation, but to obtain it without prayer would be rare, even miraculous. However, there is no limit to God's power, and His merciful love surpasses all His other works" (Guigo II, *The Ladder of Monks*).

## The Holistic Nature of *Lectio Divina*

Different faculties come to the forefront in each stage of *lectio divina*. Just as it is artificial to distinguish precisely between the stages of *lectio divina*, so the various faculties engaged [sensate (reading), mental (meditation), unconscious mind (meditation), affective/emotions (prayer), spiritual (prayer, contemplation), and in a group, social/relational] are likewise intertwined and not readily divisible. This integration yields a positive by-product: usage of all our faculties during *lectio* translates to spontaneous incorporation in daily life. *Lectio*, like Catholic and biblical spirituality in general, is not compartmentalized. The habits and attitudes we cultivate naturally spill over to the rest of our life.

This holistic or integrated characteristic also applies on the moral level: the way we practice love of God, self, and neighbor with our whole heart, mind, and strength (cf. Mk 12:28-34), and how it forms us as whole persons according to Jesus' commands (cf. Mt 5:48).

## Retreat

I use the term "retreat" as both a noun and a verb. It is a description of the purpose and mentality underlying *lectio* as well as an informal stage or activity. A retreat is a traditional spiritual practice of getting away (retreating) for a day, a weekend, or more to reflect on God's word and discern His activity in your life. You can call it an expanded Sabbath or a spiritual vacation.

*Lectio* is meant to be a periodic Sabbath moment bridged to our activities and daily life through application of the "word" we have received. It is a retreat from our hustle-bustle existence for purposes of slowing down, taking stock of life, and discerning God's will and initiative. Even a few minutes can be a regenerating oasis of calm. View *lectio* as a retreat rather than a burden. It is time to be refreshed and renewed by God's word.

## Relaxing

Traditionally, relaxing has not been articulated as a stage of *lectio divina*. However, given the hectic nature of modern life and cultural pressures working against the *shalom* (peace/wholeness) that God offers us, it seems prudent to articulate relaxing as a preparatory stage.

As with a couple who have been away from each other for awhile, we need time to get used to a more immediate experience of God's presence, and temporarily let go of anxieties and distractions. Otherwise we will not be able to tune in to God's subtle *modus operandi*, the still, small voice (cf. 2 Kings 19:12).

To use a eucharistic image, when you share a special meal with someone, you usually don't jump right in to an intense discussion. (At Mass we build up to the consecration.) You get an initial reading on yourself, your counterpart, and the situation, and then enter into a mode of interaction conducive to a deeper engagement of mind and heart.

Our ancestors knew how to relax and slow down. They didn't live in a secular, materialistic, productivity-oriented culture like ours. They didn't need to articulate relaxation as a stage because they did it naturally. We need to remind ourselves and take steps to facilitate relaxation. Examples of such include deep breathing, guided imagery, and awareness exercises. Physical exercise is also helpful for getting emotional toxins out of our system and clearing our mind.

Relaxation is neither an escape nor a shirking of responsibilities. It is a spiritual form of leisure that is not akin to "wasting time." By giving ourselves time to relax and become conscious of God's welcome and presence, we're more disposed to hear His word and receive His graces.

## Reading/Listening/Sensing (*Lectio*)

*Lectio divina* is unlike most styles of reading you have experienced. You read slowly and rhythmically, almost the antithesis of speed-reading. You'll eventually settle into a rhythm and pace that facilitates internalization of God's word.

If feasible, read aloud or in an almost imperceptible whisper or undertone. Sometimes your energy level or the circumstances dictate that you read silently, but if at all possible try speaking or whispering the word. Ancient physicians prescribed reading as a form of exercise. When you try reading aloud, you'll know why. It requires effort and energy!

When you read aloud, you use all of your senses. Yes, even taste and smell. The medieval monks who practiced *lectio divina* spoke of tasting the word by savoring its sweetness and mouthing or speaking the words in a careful, reverential way.

Can you smell God's word? Literally no, but metaphorically yes. Beginning with St. Paul, spiritual writers have spoken of spirituality in terms of an aroma (cf. 2 Cor 2:15). Using our imagination, we can sense the terrain on which Jesus traversed, the fragrance of the flowers he admired, and the smell of farm animals, laborers, travelers, and fishermen.

This engagement of the senses is one reason I emphasized relaxing as a necessary preparation. The more relaxed and present you are, the less impaired your senses will be, and the more readily you will engage them.

As a holistic side effect, using all of your senses engages your imagination, and this naturally translates to the way you experience life, i.e., more sensately and holistically. With greater familiarity with *lectio divina* and the Bible, you will have a fuller experience of the sensate dimensions of the text and life.

## Spiritual Grazing: Nibbling on the Word

In practicing *lectio divina*, we're not concerned with covering a preordained amount of the Bible in one sitting. Just as an unexpected event or brief interpersonal encounter can have significant repercussions and evoke intense reactions and reflection, so a small portion of the Bible can go a long way.

We typically begin with a small passage of Scripture. Precisely how much is not important. We read until some word, verse, image, theme, or perhaps a related personal experience or biblical text strikes us. We then take in and reflect on that stimulus. See *The St. Joseph Guide to the Bible* for recommended reading plans with respect to the Bible.

Good things come in small passages. One of the side effects of sampling a small portion of Scripture is the humility and calm it instills. It slows us down. We lose any pretense of being a master of the word or the world. In the spirit of Psalm 131, we don't set our eyes on the heights of personal gratification. Rather, we satisfy ourselves to be nurtured by the Lord. A small portion of Scripture, taken to heart, is more than enough to nourish and challenge us.

I use the term spiritual grazing quite literally, as the back and forth movement of the ruminant animal recalls the ancient pastoral image associated with *lectio divina* as well as the traditional Jewish practice of *shukkling*, that is, rocking back and forth in response to the energy generated by a holistic encounter with God's word. Perhaps the most familiar example of this is at the Wailing Wall in Jerusalem.

In giving our whole selves to a small portion of Scripture, we buck the consumption mentality of our times. Instead of mechanically devouring God's word and hurriedly going on to the next activity or stimulus, we savor it and let it permeate our being and influence our attitudes and actions.

What if no word stands out and we feel unmoved by the biblical passage? Don't worry about it. Accept what comes, even if it's only the slightest of inspirations or consolations (e.g., peaceful sensations; cf. Phil 4:7). *Lectio divina* isn't a results-oriented competition in which we are judged by how much Scripture speaks to us. God will provide what we need. Our job is to make time for God, offer ourselves as we are, avoid sloppiness, presumption, and lethargy, and keep at it (cf. Mt 24:46; Lk 8:15; 21:19): "Rejoice in hope, endure in affliction, persevere in prayer" (Rom 12:12).

## Meditation (*Meditatio*)

Once we have identified a portion of Scripture that speaks to us, our next step is to experience that text in all its richness. Savor and internalize it through repetitive recitation or murmuring. Pope Benedict describes it this way:

"Among the many fruits of this biblical springtime I would like to mention the spread of the ancient practice of *lectio divina* or 'spiritual reading' of Sacred Scripture. It consists in pouring over a biblical text for some time, reading it and rereading it, as it were, 'ruminating' on it as the Fathers say and squeezing from it, so to speak, all its 'juice,' so that it may nourish meditation and contemplation and, like water, succeed in irrigating life itself" (Benedict XVI, November 6, 2005).

In biblical and patristic times, the most frequent image associated with meditation was of a cow or goat *ruminating* (chewing its cud). Psalm 1:2 advocates murmuring or reciting God's word repeatedly.

## Utilizing Our Memories

Our memories are not as active or as developed as our ancestors'. Without the benefit of communication storage media, they had more need and practice. Most people today can remember only a small portion of Scripture. Repetitively reciting Scripture enlarges our capacity for God's word, just as it did our ancestors'. Murmuring or whispering the words repetitively can ingrain them in our memory. Not only do we remember it better, but we internalize and assimilate it, making it a part of us.

One byproduct of becoming a consistent practitioner of *lectio divina* is that of increased awareness of the potentialities of our faculties, many of which are often underutilized (e.g., our memories, and subconscious mind), and of God and the Church's desire that we develop ourselves to the fullest. *Lectio divina* engages our whole self in surrender to the divine will and for the good of ourselves, the Church, and the world. Accordingly, it helps us fulfill our individual and communal potential.

In his March 26, 1967 encyclical *Populorum Progressio* ("On the Development of Peoples"), Pope Paul VI observed:

"In the design of God, every man is called upon to develop and fulfill himself, for every life is a vocation.

"By the unaided effort of his own intelligence and his will, each man can grow in humanity, can enhance his personal worth, can become more a person. However, this self-fulfillment is not something optional. Just as the whole of creation is ordained to its Creator, so spiritual beings should of their own accord orientate their lives to God, the first truth and the supreme good. Thus it is that human fulfillment constitutes, as it were, a summary of our duties.

". . . But there is much more: this harmonious enrichment of nature by personal and responsible effort is ordered to a further perfection. By reason of his union with Christ, the source of life, man attains to new fulfillment of himself, to a transcendent humanism which gives him his greatest possible perfection: this is the highest goal of personal development."

In his will, Paul VI offered this poignant reflection:

"Why have I not studied, explored, admired sufficiently this place in which life unfolds? What unpardonable distraction, what reprehensible superficiality!"

Beginning with his first encyclical *Redemptor Hominis* ("Redeemer of Man"), and continuing throughout his pontificate, Pope John Paul II focused on the moral, spiritual, and developmental ramifications of human dignity, which was to become his signature theme. His theology of the body teachings (weekly addresses conducted from September, 1979 through November, 1984) were a profound theological anthropology of human development and fulfillment as it relates to human sexuality. The documents of Vatican II, particularly *Gaudium et Spes* ("The Pastoral Constitution on the Church in the Modern World"), and subsequent magisterial teaching likewise emphasized human fulfillment, wellness, and spirituality in all its dimensions, with the recent focus on *lectio divina* being a logical development of this theme. The holistic and dialogical nature of *lectio divina* helps us fulfill the first and second commandments (cf. Mt 22:34-40), which mandate the gift of our whole and true selves to God and neighbor.

## Inspired Input

What else happens when we repeat God's word? Like a computer, we feed our mind and heart positive input. The better the data or programming we receive, the greater the likelihood of positive output. This is why we spend time during the reading stage seeking a personally meaningful word. Unlike a motivational tape containing subliminal (subconscious) messages, *we chose* this word, its personal meaning and energy heightened by its divine imprint. God's input helps us assimilate and live our resolutions.

What happens when we internalize God's word? We open ourselves to God's healing touch. We enable God to penetrate our subconscious and reform the negative programming (thoughts, images, and memories) that has been with us from childhood. He replaces them with words and images of consolation and encouragement. Through a spiritual process analogous to that of osmosis, inspired attitudes, values, and behavior patterns gradually replace negative ones.

## Applying the Word to Life

Rumination is the transitional stage from reading to meditation. It then leads to discursive meditation, moving from thought to thought, or reminiscence, recalling other texts or life experiences. The ultimate objective of these is personal application: What bearing does the word have on our life? To what concrete actions and attitudes are God and the passage calling us?

Lest the linear, methodical way I have described this process mislead you, remember that *lectio divina* is a dialogical encounter and thus is not subject to rigid categorization. Analytical folks like me may find the aforementioned flow description helpful, while more spontaneous, contemplative types may be burdened by it. Remember that regardless of our perspective and preferences, the Spirit directs the process, and thus these descriptions are purely for instructional and guidance purposes.

One of the wonderful aspects of Catholicism is the way that it holds structure and spontaneity, creed and charism, nature and grace in a healthy tension, thereby remaining both inclusive and universal. This solidity, the actual term used by Popes Paul VI and John Paul II (reference *Ecclesiam Suam* and *Redemptor Hominis*) to describe the mission of the Church in light of Vatican II, is fundamental to *lectio divina* in that we do not practice it in a vacuum. Whenever my *lectio divina* time becomes dry and directionless, I consult Church documents, spiritual books, fellow Catholics and clergy, and avail myself of Eucharist and Confession. Prayer, devotions, and Bible-reading should always be done in connection with rather than in isolation from the Church.

## Little Victories

"Who would not admit that it is only little by little that a human being succeeds in establishing priorities, putting together many tendencies so as to arrange them harmoniously in that virtue of marital chastity wherein the couple find their full human and Christian fulfillment" (Pope Paul VI, May 4, 1970, Address to the Teams of Our Lady).

Most of the time the Spirit inspires us to make little improvements that we can implement in daily life. This applies to *lectio* as well as to life. There is a learning curve with *lectio* as with most activities. It takes time to find our rhythm, but we never really get into a comfortable groove, at least in my opinion. God, circumstances, and our own weakness and instability come together to make our practice of *lectio* a constant challenge. Like marriage, our dialogue with God has its ups and downs. Our love and fidelity is manifested most during the difficult times, when we hang in there and persevere amid dryness and disillusionment.

I try not to get down on myself or God during those times where my *lectio* is dry and arduous. I simply keep at it, consigning results to God and satisfying myself with efforts. I know that in God's time He will make the Scriptures come alive for me, perhaps during a life experience which will bring to mind a biblical text I have practiced *lectio* on. Recalling Proverbs 24:16 "... a righteous man falls seven times, and rises again," I take consolation in knowing that even St. Joseph, and in a unique way, Mary, had their opaque moments.

Focusing on manageable growth and change keeps us humble and busy. If we set our sights on grandiose, large-scale change in a short period of time, we might not respond properly or even get around to it. I discuss these "little victories" and their developmental, therapeutic, and transformational possibilities in my books *Personal Energy Management* and *Calming the Stormy Seas of Stress.*

The research and writings of Dr. Karl E. Weick, professor of organizational behavior at the Ross School of Business at the University of Michigan, on the subject of "small wins" may also be helpful. This concept has been used in corporations, schools, and institutions throughout the world, as well as by individuals in demanding fields such as athletics where success is often achieved by the narrowest of margins and little things make a big difference.

The "little way" spirituality underlying little victories is that of a doctor of the Church, St. Thérèse Lisieux. Her attention to and promotion of humble, unassuming, manageable acts of kindness and fidelity to God's will, word, and providence in daily life inspire us to achieve our own "little victories." Little victories are a practical, manageable vehicle for applying the word we receive in *lectio divina.*

## Personalizing the Word

When we make the word personal and practical by applying it to our life, we enable it to take root and transform us, day by day. It grows like the mustard seed (cf. Mk 4:30-32), imperceptible except to the eyes of faith, and dependent upon the virtues of patience and perseverance. We might reflect on the following, and perhaps include them as a daily entry in our journal:

- *What are the little ways of living the word I received in* lectio *today?*
- *What small steps of healing, growth, or outreach are accessible to me?*
- *What attitudes and actions will support or impede my practicing the little way of little victories with* lectio?
- *What biblical texts affirm the little way of discipleship and development?*

## Accessing Our Memory and Imagination

Meditation involves historical and creative elements as well. The Bible takes on another dimension when we engage our memory and imagination. We broaden our horizons chronologically, intellectually, emotionally, and spiritually.

Reminiscence, the phenomena of one biblical text evoking recollection of another, also applies to life experiences: a biblical text can remind us of a personal experience, and vice-versa. Our memory and ability to make connections help us integrate the text we are engaging with life and related parts of the Bible. The Spirit facilitates a fluid, rhythmic dialogue between the Bible and life, with us as protagonists in the drama.

Our imagination can engage our senses and transport us to the biblical scene, or project it to our circumstances. In this way we participate personally in the text, rather than as an observer: "I had heard of you by word of mouth, but now my eye has seen you" (Job 42:5). Job's personal conversion and transformation (cf. Job 42:6) is a paradigm of the *lectio* process.

## Job's Dramatization of *Lectio Divina*

The book of Job is a poetic narrative of *lectio divina* in which the protagonist goes through its stages in search of meaning and restoration. I discuss this in detail in my book *The Art and Vocation of Caring for People in Pain.* The dialogical encounter with God that culminates in the theophany (i.e., a divine manifestation, in Job's case, out of the whirlwind) shows the authenticity and efficacy of Job's wrestling with the word of Scripture and life even when the bystander religious experts find his language theologically intolerable. Job demonstrates the practice of reminiscence in relating his current situation to relevant biblical texts and life experiences.

Job and fellow skeptics and lamenters such as Qoheleth and Jeremiah offer us texts that can serve as inspired springboards for bringing our pain to God. Archbishop Fulton J. Sheen pointed out the substantial difference between whining or griping to others and complaining to God. The former serves no ultimate purpose other than a release of tensions, whereas the latter accomplishes the aforementioned and puts us in dialogue with God, through which He can divert our attention from our narrow focus and open us up to divine insight and healing.

## *Lectio* Lesson from the Pope

On November 25, 1970, Pope Paul VI gave a memorable address on people's responsiveness to God:

"Some laugh; others say to Him: we will hear You another time, as they said to Saint Paul in the Areopagus at Athens (Acts 17:32-33). However, someone there has listened, and always listens, and has perceived that in that plaintive but assured voice there can be distinguished two singular and most sweet accents, which resound wonderfully in the depths of their spirits: one is the accent of truth and the other is the accent of love."

From this I derive three essential lessons for our practice and sharing of *lectio divina.* First, *lectio* is not a numbers game either on an individual or communal basis. Its efficacy is not determined by how much textual territory we cover or insights we gain, but rather how obedient, faithful, and responsive we are. When I share *lectio* with others, for ecumenical or evangelization purposes, I try to remain undaunted in the face of negative or disappointing results. As St. Paul says, we humans may plant the seed of the Gospel, but it is God who makes it grow. Further, I don't judge myself or others, but rather leave such to God, hopeful of His commendation (cf. 1 Cor 3:1-9; 4:1-5). Likewise it is not how many people show up at parish Bible-sharing groups that matters most, but the disposition and actions of those who are present.

My own experience at Bible-sharing groups that utilize the *lectio divina* model is that out of curiosity, interest, or sincere intention many people will show up at the first or first few sessions. However, with the passage of time and the lack of fulfillment of some of the participants' expectations, and perhaps boredom or discouragement, attendance gradually dwindles, until you get down to a core group. I have often learned much from those who remain faithful to the group and process. Like the Apostles who remain after the bread of life discourse, they recognize that Jesus is the One to turn to and remain with (cf. Jn 6:67-69). I learn something from my own and others' humble perseverance and satisfaction with little victories, especially in the face of discouragement or obstacles.

The second and third lessons are that truth and love are the criteria by which I measure my *lectio divina* experience. Am I being honest with God, myself, and others? Like Job, am I being present and laying it all on the line, bringing my whole self to God? Am I open to the truth as revealed to me by Scripture and the Church, or do I seek affirmation of my agenda and presuppositions? Am I satisfied with God's love, and am I willing to reciprocate, particularly with respect to my neighbor? If we give our hearts and minds to God during *lectio*, we can be free of anxiety and scrupulosity over rituals, procedures, and expectations connected with *lectio*, and simply engage God in honest and prayerful dialogue.

I'll deal with one of the most common questions and concerns with respect to *lectio*, "How much time should I devote to *lectio* in a given session?" in the next chapter in the context of our chaotic schedules and culture.

## Prayer (*Oratio*)

Suppose you have read God's word sensitively and attentively, internalized it through repetition and reflection, and made it practical through application. These stimuli naturally evoke an emotional and spiritual reaction known as prayer or the active dimension of spiritual dialogue. Its tone and thrust varies with the person and circumstance. You might lament (in my case, rant and rave in Job-like fashion when life becomes difficult), ask God for something, praise Him, engage Him in conversation, or simply be with Him. All of this is prayer.

A traditional term used to describe the emotional content of prayer is the affective dimension: How am I *affected* by this biblical or life passage/event?

If you don't share your emotions with God and others, they are liable to be released in potentially destructive ways such as inappropriate compensatory behavior, addictions, projections onto others, or physical ailments such as ulcers.

## *Lectio* on the Psalms

The psalms are particularly efficacious for *lectio* because they capture the whole gamut of human emotions and experience in a succinct and poetic manner. The arrangement of the psalms in the lectionary, Liturgy of the Hours, and missal is particularly conducive to *lectio* due to the typical correspondence between the psalm and the surrounding readings. The psalm often gives vivid expression to key points in the Old and New Testament readings, and its personal tone, prayerful spirit, and open-ended and inclusive language inspire us to make the psalm, or at least part of it, our own. Such personalization includes uniting our words and sentiments with the psalm and letting the Spirit pray within us.

The beginning of mature prayer is the recognition of the poverty and dependence of our prayer on the Spirit (cf. Rom 8:26-27). The Lord uses children as an example of the citizens of the kingdom, because of their innocence and receptivity, reminding us that we must accept our poverty before God as a condition to praying in the Spirit. As with Moses at the burning bush, the *lectio* dialogue is always initiated by God but it requires movement and cooperation on our part. Only when God saw Moses moving toward the burning bush did God call out to him.

We can use the psalms as our prayer book, liturgically either with the Liturgy of the Hours or the lectionary (either prayerful listening to the readings at Mass or in private or communal *lectio*), or by reading the psalms in either random, thematic, literary classification, or sequential order.

The Liturgy of the Hours comes with the highest recommendation even though it is challenging and the four-volume set is expensive. However, condensed versions are available (see the Bibliography), and in the spirit and manner of *lectio* one need not feel obligated to engage all the readings, petitions, or prayers in a given sitting or day. The little way of spirituality can apply to the Liturgy of the Hours as well as the lectionary.

Personally, I prefer the lectionary, because after writing twelve books on *lectio* and teaching it throughout the world I have still not found the time, energy, commitment, self-discipline, and patience to pray the (divine) office (its traditional name), and I also find the lectionary more manageable. Both provide a structure that is very important in our chaotic world, where an abundance of stimuli threaten to distract us from the most important things in life, including prayer and *lectio*.

The psalms are the prayer book of the Church. Their sufficiency is underscored by the lack of a comparable volume in the New Testament. The psalms' poetic structure, profound wisdom, moving inspirations, and manageable length make them digestible in small portions and thereby conducive to the little way and little victories approach.

There are psalms for every emotion, circumstance, and experience. Just one expression or verse from the psalm can be a *lectio* word to bridge to your day and use as a centering point. Make the psalms your prayer book, utilize them in conjunction with the biblical reading plan that works for you (see chapter two of *The St. Joseph Guide to the Bible*), and incorporate them into your sacramental life, accessing them in the Sacraments of Eucharist and Reconciliation as well as marriage and its sustenance, for which the psalms, Song of Songs, and the creation narratives (cf. Gen 1-3) and derivative passages (cf. Mt 19:3-12; Mk 10:2-10; Col 3:16-18; Eph 5:21—6:4; Tob 8:4-9) are ideally suited.

## Perseverance Can Be a Prayer

As the psalms affirm and exemplify (almost every psalm includes some form of praise of God, including the lament psalms; only Psalms 88 and 137 end on a sour note), the ideal is to include some element, however small, of praise, even if you're feeling low. If you don't feel capable of praising God at the moment, you can pray for the *desire* to praise Him. Similarly, if you are having trouble forgiving someone who has hurt you, you can pray for the *desire* to forgive them. By persevering in prayer and good works, God can break down the walls around your heart.

Affirming your faith in God and not resorting to bitterness or immorality when you have negative or ambivalent feelings towards Him or your life situation is infinitely pleasing to God, even if you don't feel good about it. The late Jesuit theologian Karl Rahner observed that a sign of the Holy Spirit's presence is when you do something good, yet you don't have a positive, tingly feeling about it. This means that God deems you capable of doing good for its own sake, in the original Hebrew being "good for nothing" (i.e., unconditionally, disinterestedly), independent of the reward that might accompany such goodness. This was the subject of the debate in Job (cf. Job 1:9; 2:3-6).

Saints such as Paul of the Cross, John of the Cross, and Thérèse of Lisieux experienced feelings of abandonment and in some cases depression. We now know that Charles de Foucauld and Mother Teresa shared their plight, which should not surprise us. External appearances can be deceiving. Many people who undergo intense suffering emulate Jesus' words in the Sermon on the Mount regarding not making a public spectacle of their mortification (cf. Mt 6:16-18).

Prov 3:11-12 and Heb 12:5-6 warn us that God disciplines those whom He loves. But why does the ordeal have to be so painful and protracted? What enables them to remain faithful is the biblical and pneumatic reassurance that they will persevere amid trials, and thereby emerge like fire-tested gold (cf. 1 Pet 1:6-7). Admittedly, this is little consolation in the midst of testing, and the Bible itself recognizes this (cf. Heb 12:11).

When we experience desolation amid prayer, and have not been lax about our faith or morality, we should recognize that we are in good company and invite the saints' and the Spirit's intercession (cf. Rom 8:26-27), along with the support and guidance of trusted confidants.

## Contemplation (*Contemplatio*)

Prayer is the active side of the *lectio* dialogue. The receptive side is contemplation. At the risk of oversimplification, *prayer* is offering ourselves to God, while *contemplation* is receiving Him. Together they result in a consecration of the person to God similar to that which occurs at the Eucharist. The traditional and popular term for contemplation, "simple presence," recalls our disposition towards the real presence of Jesus in the Eucharist. Section 21 of *Dei Verbum*, the Vatican II document on the Bible, speaks of receiving the bread of life at the table both of God's word and Christ's body.

## Contemplation as a Doorway to Intimacy

Contemplation is a time for being and listening. When we are still and quiet, we are better able to hear God.

Contemplation is like sitting with your significant other. After sharing words and affections, you bask in each other's presence. Words are no longer necessary. Your goal is not achievement or activity, but intimacy and presence. You slow down, desist from frenetic activity, listen, temporarily let go of anxieties and concerns, and bask in God's arms. You rest from the energy-consuming activities in the *lectio* process. The strenuous part of your exercise completed, you cool down in God's presence.

## Resting in the Lord

Contemplation is the epitome and consummation of the Sabbath experience that is *lectio divina*. We rest and spend time with God. We need to recharge and re-center ourselves more than just weekly. Sabbath moments fill us with divine wisdom and peace. They regenerate and empower us to live the word we have received. We come full circle in the *lectio* process, relaxing receptively before God after the energy-consuming activities of *lectio*, just as we relax in the initial retreat stage in recuperation from our apostolic endeavors and life experiences.

The journey continues. *Lectio* is a lifestyle and a spiritual path rather than simply a devotional activity. How often we find en route that we get more than we bargained for. Beware what you ask for, because you may get it!

Lest you get discouraged when you have difficulty sitting still with God, recognize that I (and many others) have a similar problem. Slowing down and resting in God is difficult for persons in western cultures, where ideologies (i.e., materialism, fundamentalism) and idolatries (e.g., consumerism) abound, compulsive activity is the norm, and autonomy (rugged individualism) is romanticized and glorified. The idea of letting God take over for a few moments is a shock to our system. We can overcome both internal and external obstacles through a commitment to quiet time and trust in God's fidelity.

## Consolation (*Consolatio*)

Consolation is not an activity of *lectio*. It is a fruit of the Spirit (cf. Gal 5:22-23) induced by *lectio* and other graced spiritual exercises. It can occur at any point in the *lectio* process, but often ensues during contemplation, when we cease activities and move into receptive mode.

Consolation is necessary for maintaining our enthusiasm for reading and living the Bible. It is essential that we go to the Bible expecting God to nourish us spiritually: "But without faith it is impossible to please him, for whoever comes to God must believe that he exists and that he rewards those who seek him" (Heb 11:6; cf. Lk 11:13).

## Defining Consolation

Consolation is not an ethereal feeling of well-being and contentment. It rarely includes an extra-sensory experience of God's presence, like Moses at the burning bush (cf. Ex 3:2-4) or Elijah in the desert (cf. 1 Kings 19:11-18). Usually it is much more subtle and ordinary.

Consolation is a graced (freely given by God) state of "the shalom (peace and wholeness) that surpasses all understanding" (cf. Phil 4:7). It is better *experienced* than described: "In the same way, even the Spirit helps us in our weakness. For we do not know how to pray as we should, but the Spirit intercedes for us with sighs too deep for words" (Rom 8:26).

Consolation has traditionally been understood as the comfort and peace that is a gift of the Spirit to those who love God and do as He commands (cf. Jn 14:16). The Bible's most thorough discussion of the gifts of the Spirit is 1 Cor 12—14. Discernment of spirits is mentioned in 1 Cor 12:10, 1 Jn 4:1-6, Jas 1:12-18, and 1 Thes 5:19-22, and discernment in general in Heb 5:11-14, 1 Cor 2:6-16, and 1 Pt 2:1-2.

## Action (*Actio*)

Despite the consoling reassurances that often accompany contemplation, we can't depend on God for everything: we have to do our part and cooperate with Him. We must share and practice what we have received.

In the action stage, the *lectio* of Scripture (revelation) encounters the *lectio* of life (providence), and the dialogue of salvation (a seminal expression of Popes Paul VI and John Paul II articulated prominently in their first encyclicals) emerges.

Action, the consummating stage of *lectio*, is the way we bear witness to the word and give it life. It is implicit in the other stages, as each requires us to engage in some sort of action. Even the most receptive stage, contemplation, requires us to make a conscious effort to sit still.

Action is the most exciting, beneficial, and difficult aspect of *lectio divina*. We encounter the strongest resistance from ourselves and others when we try to implement God's word. Talking about or conceptualizing the word does not threaten the world, the flesh, and the devil nearly as much as living it (cf. 1 Jn 2:16).

Even Moses was susceptible to telling others to trust in God while he was slow to act:

"And Moses said to the people, 'Fear not, stand firm, and see the salvation of the Lord, which he will work for you today; for the Egyptians whom you see today, you shall never see again. The Lord will fight for you, and you have only to be still.' The Lord said to Moses, 'Why do you cry to me? Tell the people of Israel to go forward'" (Ex 14:13-15). (Note the integration of action and stillness representative of *lectio divina*.)

## The Continuity and Versatility of *Lectio Divina*

*Lectio divina* is ongoing and organic. It is the process through which God's word becomes the seed that bears fruit in abundance (cf. Mk 4:8). It reveals itself in life through the mystery of providence (God's initiative and intervention in human affairs).

Many spiritual exercises have their roots in or are related to *lectio*; it is a seminal spiritual, therapeutic, and developmental process. As we apply the wisdom and directives we experience in *lectio*, we understand God's word and ourselves in a deeper way.

*Lectio* isn't a static, mechanical process that ends with the completion of our quiet time. Rather, it is a dynamic, evolving experience of living God's word amid human resistance and limitations. Life is the cauldron in which God's word mixes with providence and our response, and personal and collective salvation history unfolds. *Lectio* is a privileged participation in this dialogue of salvation, in collaboration with the Sacraments and other dimensions in the life of the Church.

*Lectio divina* is a relatively simple and natural process, although it is multi-dimensional and has a lot of nuances and applications. Feedback from readers and those I teach and guide indicate that practical examples are very helpful. They want to see how, given the constraints and challenges of modern life, *lectio* happens in the real world for people who don't have the time or interest to be biblical scholars or secluded contemplatives.

People respond best, and are inspired most, by real-life examples. With our conceptual and procedural foundation in place, the remainder of this book will focus on the two finest practitioners of *lectio divina*, Mary and Joseph, who learned first hand from the Source and Word Himself, Jesus.

# – Two –

## On the Run with the Word of God
## Responding to Stressful Times in Union
## with the Holy Family

### *Lectio* Review and Preview

AS discussed in chapter one, *lectio divina* is a traditional Latin term for a holistic process of prayerfully
reading and responding to God's word. Its five stages: reading / listening, meditation, prayer, contemplation, and action,
are fundamental to the spirituality of most major religions,
though theological and devotional connotations vary consid-
erably.

Because its activities are so fundamental to human spirituality and development, and God's word encompasses more than
the Bible, the process of *lectio divina* can also be applied to life
experiences and other devotional and liturgical activities. It has
a cross-cultural, non-sectarian, amorphous (adaptable to many
circumstances) dimension which makes it suitable for ecumenical dialogue and evangelization along with wellness and potential fulfillment. We'll discuss this briefly in chapter five.

In the early and medieval Church, *lectio divina* was also
applied to the writings of the Church Fathers, which typically
draw extensively from Scripture. *Lectio* (often abbreviated to
such) can be used with other spiritual writings, especially those
grounded in the Bible such as spiritual classics or magisterial
documents.

As discussed in Fr. Dysinger's article in the appendix, the
process of *lectio divina* can also be applied to devotions (e.g.,
the Rosary, Stations of the Cross, the Jesus Prayer), the

Sacraments, and life, including our personal and communal salvation history. In chapter five you will learn a complementary developmental model which will help you identify and respond effectively to divine or human signs using the *lectio* process. *Lectio's* pliable nature enables it to complement a multitude of spiritual exercises and activities, as well as life experiences.

An advantage of practicing *lectio divina* with magisterial writings is that you benefit from the competent and authoritative interpretations and applications of the Church, and thereby have a greater assurance of understanding the literal and applied meaning of the Bible properly.

As you will learn throughout this book, *lectio divina* is not a method, but a process, dialogue, and lifestyle. It operates from a sacramental perspective, that is, emphasizing the divine word and mystery that permeates and sanctifies all of life. Accordingly, it seems fitting to view *lectio* from the root of that mystery, the Holy Family.

## Where We've Been and Where We're Going

In the first chapter, I offered a traditional introduction to *lectio divina*: what it is, how it evolved, its components, and how it is practiced. More than enough to get you started. You'll learn as you go. Because it is such a natural, simple, and straightforward model, you don't need an inordinate amount of conceptual preparation.

I didn't delve too deeply into *lectio's* history because knowledge of such is helpful, but not essential, to its practice, particularly for beginners. Books listed in the bibliography and the articles in the appendix provide additional historical background.

What you received in the previous chapter will get you started and, along with the forthcoming chapters, will sustain you. We all need guidance and support, and especially examples. Good role models. Proof that it can be done; hope without illusion. Encouragement. That's what much of the rest of this book is about. You can view it as a case study on *lectio divina* in action, featuring the unparalleled authorities. You can't get better teachers than the Holy Family.

## The Dynamics of the Holy Family

We will focus on Mary and Joseph because Jesus, as the Son of God, is a special case. Nonetheless He is part of the Holy Family, and no doubt taught and learned from them. We might term this relationship and reaction an intimate spiritual osmosis, an interactive seeping in and assimilation of love and truth, incarnate in Jesus, the primary word of God (cf. 1 Jn 1:1-18).

The Gospel of Luke stated that Jesus grew in wisdom and grace before men (cf. Lk 2:40, 50-52), so we know that Jesus had to develop just like the rest of us. Mary and Joseph were a significant part of Jesus' growth, and in turn were affected by it.

The parallel to our lives is apparent: When you encounter the word of God, whether in the Bible or in the person of Jesus, the suffering person (with whom Jesus identifies; cf. Mt 25:31-46), or in the Church, Christ's body, you are affected, even if it is not immediately noticeable. You can't stay the same, for the Word demands a decision. *Lectio divina* helps us to discern God's will, make good decisions, and tap into God's healing and transforming power.

Mary and Joseph are ideal models in terms of their attitudes and actions. On a strictly literal and socio-cultural level, we don't observe many parallels between their lives and ours. They lived in a vastly different culture. However, the challenges they faced were very similar to ours, as discussed below.

## The Word on the Loose: Under the Gun and on the Run

The descriptions, principles, and procedures offered in the previous chapter sound good in theory, but putting them into practice is another matter. The obstacles we encounter both within ourselves and in our circumstances complicate what in essence is a simple process. We have to live with these complexities and make the best of them, including turning them to the good with God's help.

Everyone will respond to this challenge differently, but there are common elements that can be identified, and most of them are present in the lives of our model, the Holy Family. Let's take stock of our lives in the shadow of Scripture and the Spirit, and see what light they shed on us.

## The Pace of Modern Life

For most persons, life in the twenty-first century is lived at a rapid, pressurized pace. It seems like there is always something to do, some expectation to fulfill, and time and opportunities are scarce. We're always looking for that elusive break or respite that never seems to come. Instead of shortening the work-week, as predicted, technology, along with the downturn in the global economy and the breakdown of the nuclear family, have lengthened it. Due to beepers and cell phones, we are always on call.

In reading the Bible and other historical narratives, we quickly learn that we are not the only generation to operate in such circumstances. Life waits and simplifies for no one. Accordingly, we had best adapt and make the best of our situation.

The word of God helps us do this in an integral way because it too maintains a fast pace. In 2 Thes 3:1, St. Paul invites prayers that the word of God speed forward and be glorified through the cooperation of believers. We contribute to the word of God's dynamism by our responsiveness.

Keeping up with God's word requires us to shed ourselves of unnecessary encumbrances (cf. Heb 12:1) and get on board, taking consolation that ultimately God is in the driver's seat, unless we obstinately dislodge Him, at which point He will regretfully oblige us, though He will continually make overtures to regain our hearts. Like a spurned lover (see Hos 1—3; 2 Tim 2:13), God never quits on us.

In addition to the physical, mental, and emotional costs, there are also aesthetic, developmental, and communication encumbrances related to our fast-paced, pressurized lives. We often feel that we can't find the time and resources to live, love, and develop properly. We become marginalized by superficialities, trivialities, oppressive structures, and ever-present demands and constraints. Life, and seemingly God, waits for no one.

At least three people would disagree with the last conclusion. Jesus, Mary, and Joseph know that God waits for us even when He keeps us on the run. In fact, while He draws and prods us onward, He stays by our side, infinitely patient. He is always concerned with the lost sheep and those who struggle to keep up the pace.

However, this doesn't mean that He makes it easy on us or passively tolerates us dragging our feet. To the contrary, hoping to get our attention, He often allows our burdens to increase even when we already feel overwhelmed.

If you want biblical testimony on this point, we know who to consult: Joseph, the guardian and head of the Holy Family. Like his son, he reminds us that authority need not confer rank or privilege. Rather, from a biblical and Catholic perspective, it is constituted by service, and not necessarily in the way we foresee or prefer.

## Living with Uncertainty

With God, we never know who or what is next. And while this is certainly true of the lives of Jesus and Mary, the Bible narrates this with respect to Joseph in an explicit and compelling way. Amid Jesus' infancy the poor fellow doesn't say anything despite being continually prevented from settling down and establishing roots. Even when he sleeps he is summoned for urgent and perilous trips. His dreams are hardly the kind he or we would hope for or invite.

Joseph experiences the word of God on the run in a literal sense. He doesn't have time for preliminaries and extensive preparations. He has to move, now. As do we, in many ways and circumstances.

For example, someone who takes care of their spouse, children, and parents (sometimes while working a full-time job!)— or anyone in need, for that matter—without being corrupted by the world, is participating explicitly in the dialogue of salvation (cf. 1 Tim 2:15). Laypersons whose vocation is secular are called to balance an apostolic lifestyle with attentiveness to prayer, spiritual devotions or exercises, and worship, the fulfillment of which would seem to put them on a fast track to sainthood! It did for the Holy Family.

Unlike professed religious, whose schedules typically include designated time for prayer, devotions, and spiritual exercises, laypersons typically have to build theirs in and take advantage of opportunities for quiet time as they become available. Joseph and Mary were in the same boat. They were busy living God's word through fidelity to His commands. As with most laypersons, their education and formation occurred in the field and on the run.

We learn how to keep pace with God's word and life by slowing down, using the principles outlined in the Bible: e.g., observance of the Sabbath, periodic prayer and worship times, and appreciation of nature and each other. The Bible is not designed for speed reading, and neither is this book. To quote Gandhi, "There is more to life than increasing its speed." Take your time. When you dialogue with a loved one, you don't want to be in a hurry. You'll give your beloved the time you can and what they need, because they are important.

Likewise, our gifts of time, energy, attentiveness, and presence to God, others, and ourselves (cf. Mk 6:31) enable us to get a handle on our fast-paced, pressurized lives, and entrust them responsibly to the care of a providential and mysterious God Who can help us find our way and proper pace.

*Lectio* is the great leveler: only Jesus is the master (cf. Mt 23:9). Biblical scholars and novices alike must continually open themselves to the divine initiative and prompting. The Bible and liturgy always contain something new for us, if only we are open to it. The learning and transformation process never ends.

Balancing the literal and applied meanings in the texts lets us fill in the space left by the multitude of unreported conversations and activities engaged in by the Holy Family as they moved forward with God's word. Let us ask ourselves what meaning their lives have for us in terms of our relationship with the word of God, and how they can be an asset to us as we familiarize ourselves with the Bible and the art of putting its lessons into practice.

## The Familial Nature of *Lectio Divina*

The fundamental theme of this book is the innate link between the Holy Family and our personal and communal relationship with God's word. I have been teaching and practicing *lectio divina* for over twenty-five years, and have been constantly amazed at the familial dimensions of the practice. I have seen middle school children contribute competently to adult Bible studies, and learned profound truths about parenting and marriage from couples who share the word along with their lives. I have been edified by separated and divorced persons and single parents who come alone despite great pain, disappointment, and embarrassment. What people do speaks much louder than what they say.

One of my greatest disappointments has been the general absence of older children from Bible-sharing/study groups. I realize that they are busy with sports and extracurricular activities—and video games, television, cell phones, and the internet—but the same is true of orthodox Jewish and Evangelical Protestant children, and they find time for activities that nourish the spirit. Participation in youth Bible-related activities need not exclude occasional participation in groups with an adult presence.

Youngsters need to see their religious role models in action in an intellectually challenging communal setting. Exposure of adolescents to religious formation with adults fosters maturation and potential fulfillment. If children and families can make time to watch and attend sports events. . . . Salvation is the only game we really play for keeps.

*Lectio divina* is familial first in the sense of the seminal model of Jesus, Mary, and Joseph. Second, it is the way the Church, the family of God, reads the Scriptures. Third, it can be a foundation of communication and spirituality within the nuclear and extended family. While *lectio divina* has a private devotional dimension, this must be anchored in relationships, life, and dialogue in order to be balanced and practical.

I have been helped in my *lectio* quest by the family of God on a personal, communal, and organizational level. For example, the Catholic Biblical Federation (website c-b-f.org), established by Pope Paul VI in 1969 and the largest Catholic biblical association in the world, has provided me with a treasure trove of articles on *lectio divina* by the Church's leading teachers on the subject, including several by Cardinal Martini.

When I emphasize in this book that there is no *one* way to practice *lectio divina*, I am coming from a global perspective as well as a personal and professional one. By learning how others teach and practice it, I can refine my craft. Hopefully you'll learn much about *lectio* from others as well.

There is still another, more personal, familial dimension to this book. It reflects the insights, suggestions, and support of so many mentors, colleagues, teachers, students, and readers. I have given workshops and retreats on *lectio divina* all over the world, in a variety of environments, Catholic, Protestant, healthcare, business, and education, and have learned a great deal from persons I have encountered. I have experienced many of the difficulties that you encounter, so I write as someone struggling alongside you. This interpersonal, evangelical (sharing the good news), and communal aspect is another way in which *lectio* imparts a family feel. I hope that while you are experiencing this book, and more importantly *lectio* and the Bible, you find yourself increasingly drawn into its interpersonal and technological web. *Lectio* thereby becomes a way of life rather than simply a devotional exercise.

## The St. Joseph Dimension

In honor of its namesake, this book draws upon another focus of my work and research, men's and relationship issues. Here too I have benefited from collaboration with some of the world's finest authorities on the subject. I have worked on a manuscript with best-selling author Dr. Warren Farrell (website: warrenfarrell.com) and Dr. Cornelius F. Murphy, Jr., author of *Beyond Feminism: Towards a Dialogue on Differences*. I have frequently consulted Dr. Paul Nathanson, professor at McGill University in Montreal and co-author of a trilogy of books on misandry (contempt for men) in North American culture.

Many of my books are on topics of particular interest to women (e.g., theology of the body, stress management, suffering, care-giving, journaling, and infertility), and I have had countless discussions and correspondence with female readers and workshop participants, thereby helping me to balance my masculine bias with an infusion of feminine perspectives. Thus I am hopeful that my comments on men, women, and relationship issues will have particular relevance for women as well.

## The Signs of the Times Point to Joseph and Mary

In my work on male and relationship issues both in secular and religious spheres for over two decades, I have personally witnessed the increasing marginalization of boys and men that has been recognized for years in sociological studies. Unfortunately such research and the proposed remedies are not widely disseminated to the public, and the marginalization trends are not addressed in either secular or religious environments.

Within the Church, radical or ideological feminism has been partially addressed in the 2004 Sacred Congregation for the Doctrine of the Faith document, *Letter to Bishops of the*

*Catholic Church on the Collaboration Between Men and Women in the Church and the World.* Available on the Vatican website (www.vatican.va), it makes for informative and provocative reading.

Unfortunately, this document has been practically ignored by the North American Church, at least in terms of its influence on preaching, pastoral letters and practices, and ecclesial policies. Most Catholics don't even know that the letter exists.

This is particularly tragic given that relationships between men and women are arguably more contentious in American society than anywhere else in the world. Visitors to America often make this observation, and divorce statistics and the number of "couple" conflicts that make their way into courtrooms bear this out.

The harmony within the Holy Family and the collaboration necessary for a fruitful familial experience of *lectio divina* make it imperative that we be responsive to this document and the issues it raises. The marginalization of the father in family, parish, and social life has had devastating effects on society and the Church. Sociologists and psychologists have pointed out what happens to a society when positive male images are lacking, beginning in the family. False father images emerge and exert a destructive influence on a wide scale. When a void exists politically, tyrants, phonies, and celebrities can seduce the populace and do untold harm.

Attentiveness to St. Joseph and the Holy Family is a good place to regain our bearings. We need to rediscover St. Joseph, to seek his intercession, and to reflect on the examples he and Mary gave of how to be authentic disciples of their son. It is not enough to have a superficial appreciation of and devotion to Mary and Joseph. We need to plumb the depths of how, in their humanity, they dialogued and cooperated intimately with divinity, which is also the objective of *lectio divina.* This subject merits not only an entire book, but also a whole field of study, not only with respect to Catholic and biblical spirituality but in the area of family and gender relations as well.

However, that is for the future. Now is the time for contemplation and action. It does not suffice to dwell on the Holy Family, God's word, *lectio divina*, and gender harmony in the abstract. We have to bring it to life, and make it real and personal. For this reason, I want to offer a road map to readers on the go, corresponding to the way the Holy Family began.

## Reverent Refugees

One of the most tragic consequences of war and political strife is the displacement of innocent persons and the loss of their homes. We see this on the evening news with such disconcerting regularity that we have immunized ourselves to it.

However, as Mother Teresa often observed, impoverishment is closer to home than we think. People in tumultuous family situations also experience something of the refugee lifestyle. They are not respected or accepted in their home, by their loved ones, and are forced to live a transient, marginalized existence. Sometimes coercive behaviors such as threats and manipulation of the legal system are used by loved ones to impose such a lifestyle.

This fugitive transience is how Jesus' life began. It was far from a honeymoon experience for his parents. They moved from place to place in dangerous, unfamiliar territory, without the support of their clan, never knowing what was to befall them next. In the imagery of the psalmist, God's word and providence was like a lamp unto their feet, providing not a grand blueprint or clear vision of the future but only the strength and guidance to put one foot in front of the other.

Luke's Gospel emphasizes the importance of "daily" discipleship, that is, being focused on the present and entrusting the past and future to God. In the Sermon on the Mount, Jesus goes beyond the teaching on providence that Matthew and Luke (cf. Mt 6:25-33; Lk 12:22-31) share and counsels disciples not to worry about tomorrow because the evil of the day is challenge enough (cf. Mt 6:34).

Jesus' life began under difficult circumstances, and likely remained that way. If fidelity to God's will was very difficult for the Word of God himself (Jesus) and His parents, who nurtured and were nurtured by the Word, we cannot expect it to be any different for us. The demands and difficulties that accompany God's word are clearly acknowledged throughout the Bible and Church teaching. It was a challenge for Jesus and His parents from the beginning, and we would be wise to begin or continue our journey with God's word with similar expectations.

God's word did not come to the Holy Family in a vacuum, independent of the harsh human condition, and neither does it to us. Recognizing this helps us avoid the excuses and rationalizations that threaten and inhibit our journey:

- I don't have time for the word.
- It's beyond my comprehension.
- What does it have to do with my life?
- I'm too stressed right now to dedicate myself to God's word. I have to look out for myself—no one else will. I'll lead a good life and that should be enough. I'll leave the Bible to the professional religious.
- I tried reading and applying the Bible and all it did was confuse me and complicate my life. (Join the crowd.)

The litany can go on and on. It could have for the Holy Family and the Apostles, disciples, saints, and martyrs after them, but they chose a positive, redemptive path (cf. Col 1:24) instead.

## Making Sunday a School of the Word

Slowing down during the workweek is difficult, particularly for persons in trying circumstances. Individuals working one or two jobs while maintaining a home and perhaps taking care of elderly parents and /or a family often find leisure time at a premium. It can be carved out, but there will be interruptions, many of them unavoidable. However, if we treat these intrusions as part of divine providence, we can discover God's will for us amid them.

I learned to fit in quality time for God's word through carefully cultivated time and stress transformation principles and practices that I articulated in my books, *Calming the Stormy Seas of Stress* and *Personal Energy Management*. I also published both a generic and Catholic personal organizer known as *The Personal Energy Manager Rainbow Planner*. I was supposed to have finished a book on procrastination and punctuality last week, but didn't get to it.

Despite this background, I continually have difficulty not only carving out time for God's word, but utilizing it properly once I get it. I fall asleep frequently while journaling or reflecting on the Sunday or daily readings. I get so discouraged by the dryness that I cut my time short. I take phone calls or engage in other detours that divert my attention. I do everything that I shouldn't do except give up. Instructing others does not alleviate me from the challenges my readers and students face.

## The Fruit of Perseverance

Thankfully, there is a lighter side as well. Sometimes I get the feeling right from the start of my *lectio divina* session that I am going to be "on," that is, I will pick up the various hints and clues in the texts and recognize the divine signs or prompts I receive from the Holy Spirit. However, that's not the most difficult part. Living the message is, because things never go according to plans, the spirit is willing and the flesh is weak, and there are always multiple contingencies and external factors involved. These are part of the "generosity and failure" stage of human and spiritual development discussed in chapter four.

However, these practicalities occur after my quiet time. During my fruitful quiet times I get into an interpretive groove in which the passage seems to open up before me, and I am able to make coherent connections between this and related passages in the Bible and relate them to my life. The time flows, and I can easily spend thirty, sixty, or ninety minutes on the word.

Sometimes I'll be inspired to reference a commentary on the subject in order to understand the literal sense and the passage's biblical and historical context more precisely. I try to defer such references to the end of my *lectio* time, because I know that once I start my background reading, it will be difficult to shift gears and return to the reflective *lectio divina* mode.

I am on the alert during such times for seemingly innocuous interruptions such as telephone calls or benign requests from loved ones. If the matter or call is not urgent, I politely ask for a deferral. Many prefer to let the answering machine take a message or even take the phone off the hook (and hopefully remember to put it back). Once I complete my dialogue with God and His word, I can get back to them.

Such "tuned in" times are not predictable. They just happen, often when I least expect it or most need it. Of course, they don't happen if I am undisciplined and nonchalant and make little effort, or if I am inconsistent in my attentiveness to the word. I view them as a graced and natural reward for persevering with the Bible and prayer. I don't expect or anticipate them in a presumptuous manner. Rather, I do my best in each *lectio divina* session, and when the Spirit is moving I am ready to catch the wind. To use athletic terminology, I put myself in a position to succeed.

A good analogy is marital fidelity. Periodically, faithful couples encounter times when they are tuned in to each other and their interactions flow. Often this is not expressed in words, but in actions, including intimacy. This may appear to occur randomly, but on closer inspection it is generally a byproduct of an ongoing openness, dialogue, and respect, made even more impressive and unifying when life is not going well. A key to marital longevity is riding out the storms and learning to love your partner during those times when you don't like their attitude or behavior. Negative circumstances and failed expectations have a lot to do with disaffection as well.

Imperfection and failed expectations are the universal experience of not only the spiritual life, but also human relationships, particularly close ones where more is expected and at stake. Trusting in providence rather than in our agenda and fidelity to our own and to God's word is essential to a sustained practice of both *lectio* and love.

## The Word on Sunday

Sunday can be an anchor and centering point for individuals and families committed to allocating quality time for the important persons and activities in their life, beginning with God. Sunday can be a weekly new beginning with God and each other.

There is no better day than Sunday, and source than the Sunday readings, for beginning or resuming our dialogue with God and His word. In section seven of *Dies Domini* ("On Keeping the Lord's Day Holy"), Pope John Paul II offers this word on Sunday:

"Sunday is a day which is at the very heart of the Christian life. From the beginning of my Pontificate, I have not ceased to repeat: 'Do not be afraid! Open, open wide the doors to Christ!' In the same way, today I would strongly urge everyone to rediscover Sunday: *Do not be afraid to give your time to Christ!* Yes, let us open our time to Christ, that he may cast light upon it and give it direction. He is the One who knows the secret of time and the secret of eternity, and he gives us 'his day' as an ever new gift of his love.

"The rediscovery of this day is a grace which we must implore, not only so that we may live the demands of faith to the full, but also so that we may respond concretely to the deepest human yearnings. Time given to Christ is never time lost, but is rather time gained, so that our relationships and indeed our whole life may become more profoundly human."

We could bring this passage to *lectio divina* in the context of our life and derive a multitude of insights and applications.

*Lectio divina* can be an integral factor in rediscovering the therapeutic, transformational, and unifying benefits of the Sabbath.

- *Am I willing to make time for God's word on the Lord's Day, which is designated for worship, rest, recreation, and renewal?*

- *"Time given to Christ is never time lost, but is rather time gained, so that our relationships and indeed our whole life may become more profoundly human." What application does this papal statement have to my life? Does it correspond to or contradict my experience?*

## How Much Time?

John Paul II rightly asserts that time given to Christ is time gained, but he doesn't specify practical guidelines. Popes tend to leave such details to bishops, pastors, and the individual, who are closer to the situation and can reason and respond more precisely.

The best advice I have heard on the subject was that of the late Fr. Basil Pennington, who pioneered the practice of Centering Prayer while also writing a fine book on *lectio divina* (and many other topics, including Mary). With reference to Centering Prayer and particularly beginners in the practice, he recommended three minutes twice a day, even though his confreres such as Fr. Keating were advocating twenty to thirty minutes a day.

Centering Prayer was developed by the monks of Spencer Abbey, near Worcester, Massachusetts, in the 1970s, and it began being disseminated nationally in the 1980s. It is based on the teachings of the unknown fourteenth century author of *The Cloud of Unknowing*. As the Centering Prayer movement grew, one of its initiators and most prominent teachers, Fr. Thomas Keating, OSCO, increasingly discussed Centering Prayer within the context of *lectio divina*, and particularly as a way of practicing the contemplation stage of *lectio*. Situating it firmly in the monastic contemplative tradition helped avoid eclectic digressions and balanced it with the other spiritual components of *lectio divina*.

The reason I like the standard of three minutes is that it eliminates excuses and also invites initiative, both of which are important considerations for beginners. Obviously three minutes is not enough time for a sustained practice of *lectio divina*. We're just getting started, and all of a sudden the time is up.

Beginning with the worst-case scenario of chaotic circumstances and a tight schedule (for example, a mother of small children), three minutes is an attainable goal for at least a sincere check-in with God, a brief word with Him. Hopefully, to be continued at length later. God can work with what we offer Him. Jesus didn't need much of an opening to impart an important lesson or extend an outreach. Of course, we can't be complacent and limit ourselves or God to our narrow agenda. *Lectio divina* is inherently dynamic, and is not amenable to compartmentalization.

Something interesting happens when you allocate the three minutes. The time typically expands, and somehow you are usually able to complete your work and activities, or else you discover that they were dispensable. The peace and perspective you gain helps you recover the time providentially. Just as when you are in love a few minutes together naturally balloons, so when you let God into your life He carves out additional territory. Sometimes this is disconcerting or painful, as we need to change and let go of comfortable attachments. Our divine spouse wants all of us, and while He accepts what we offer He is always beckoning us to more.

When I teach *lectio*, I rarely pin students down to a specific amount of time, except when recalling Fr. Basil's suggestion. I don't know how you can quantify or regulate time spent on a dialogue with a lover, whether human or divine. There has to be a naturalness and flow as well as a level of commitment and discipline. As in most things Catholic and biblical, virtue is in the middle and in the balance.

Most experienced spiritual directors and teachers of *lectio* recommend ten to thirty minutes of *lectio* time for not only beginners, but experienced practitioners, with fifteen to twenty minutes being the norm. There are times when my *lectio* session has gone over ninety minutes, but that was usually on a Sunday when so-called down time was plentiful and rest was in order. Further, much of that time was taken up with background reading, which strictly speaking is not part of *lectio*, though it complements it.

In general, I find myself hovering around the norm (fifteen to twenty minutes) whenever my day is chaotic and frustrating and longer (thirty to fifty minutes) whenever I have the time, energy, and attentiveness—or my circumstances require an extensive period of reflection, discernment, and decision-making. If I nod off during my *lectio* session I simply shake it off (athletic jargon for "let it go"), and either keep reading (and sometimes, become drowsy again) or get on with my other activities, and return to *lectio* later.

Each person needs to come up with a time allocation and rhythm commensurate with their vocation and circumstances. A spiritual director or confessor can help you arrive at an acceptable pattern. While consistency is important, so is spontaneity and discernment. We have to pay attention to ourselves, the movement of the Spirit, circumstantial needs or conditions, and the guidance of the Church in arriving at a sustainable routine.

Sometimes I miss or shorten my *lectio* session for what I believe are acceptable reasons: An outreach to others, another activity compatible with my vocation and suitable at the time, illness, unavoidable contingencies, etc. I try to make it up later, or simply try again the next day. At the very least I recall the "three-minute rule" and give at least a few minutes to the Lord. When all else fails, the Lord's Prayer can be our *lectio* source, and in fact should in some measure be incorporated in each *lectio* session, as its name merits.

The inclusive, Catholic understanding of God's word is an aid in avoiding scrupulosity providing that it does not become an occasion for laxness (indulgent, undisciplined spirituality). If the time I would have spent on *lectio* has been diverted to another activity related, whether directly or indirectly, to some manifestation or application of God's word, in a sense I am still within the realm of *lectio*. Of course, I endeavor to ensure that these diversions do not become reflexive and commonplace, and recognize that there is no substitution for quiet time, personally and communally, with the Lord.

Perhaps now you understand why I normally do not go into particulars with respect to time allocations. There are too many variables and nuances. Using the "three-minute rule," you can do *lectio* in less time than it takes to sort through my guidelines. When I venture into this terrain during a presentation, I am careful to stick to generalities in order to remain reasonably on schedule. If a member of the audience brings up the aforementioned contingencies and more, it inevitably takes me and my audience on a time-consuming, but hopefully beneficial, digression.

With experience, people normally discover and refine their own rhythm, habits, and patterns with respect to *lectio*, much of it based on their capacities, vocation, and circumstances. Guidelines are particularly expedient when allied with a mature, broad understanding of morality and spirituality that enables one to navigate prudently the contingencies that ensue in the course of life and discipleship. However, a teacher cannot presume this with a general audience, and as you can see, once you start making qualifications and clarifications, others soon present themselves.

My readers can attest that it is less complicated to practice *lectio* than to explain or explore it in all its nuances. *Lectio* is a multi-faceted lifestyle of a lifetime. In the process of reading this book, I hope you find consistent occasion to practice it, so you will find out not only what *lectio* is all about, and more importantly who the Holy Family is for you, but also how the Spirit deigns to lead you in this ongoing dialogue and journey.

Time is a constraint or boundary in spiritual activities as in the rest of life, but God is also beyond time, so as your dialogue partner He can help you manage time considerations in an acceptable manner. When all else fails, bring it to prayer and perhaps consultation with a trusted confidant, and entrust it to the Lord.

## The Word of God Is on the Run

The Holy Family began their "school of the word" on the run, as exiles, as their fathers had before them. In Matthew's Gospel, they flee to Egypt and back to escape Herod's murderous intentions. In Luke's account, they respond to an ill-timed census and are consigned to a stable, as there was no room at the inn.

At times I feel rootless, in perilous transition, a victim of circumstances and bad timing, and can relate to their experience. During *lectio divina*, I contemplate their plight and the counsel and encouragement they might offer me in dealing with mine.

We should not romanticize these developments, as some Christian art does. Jesus' birthplace was dirty, uncomfortable, and potentially unsafe. Manger scenes often show loving and peaceful gazes on the face of Jesus' parents, but I imagine that concern and discomfort were also present.

Chapter 11 of the Letter to the Hebrews is a marvelous recounting of the struggles endured by the holy ones of the Old Testament. The following excerpt reminds us of the courageous faith amid suffering that must characterize our attitude towards God's word:

"What more shall I say? Time is too short for me to speak of Gideon, Barak, Samson, and Jephthah, of David and Samuel and the Prophets, who by faith conquered kingdoms, administered justice, and obtained the promises. They closed the mouths of lions, quenched raging fires, and escaped the edge of the sword. Their weakness was turned into strength as they became mighty in battle and put foreign armies to flight.

"Women received their dead back through resurrection. Others who were tortured refused to accept release in order to obtain a better resurrection. Still others were mocked and scourged, even to the point of enduring chains and imprisonment.

"They were stoned, or sawed in two, or put to death by the sword. They went about in skins of sheep or goats—destitute, persecuted, and tormented. The world was not worthy of them. They wandered about in desert areas and on mountains, and they lived in dens and caves of the earth.

"Yet all these, even though they were commended for their faith, did not receive what was promised. For God had made provision for us to have something better, and they were not to achieve perfection except with us" (Heb 11:32-40).

St. Paul reminds us of the power, joy, and suffering that accompany God's word:

". . . for our gospel came to you not only in word, but also in power and in the Holy Spirit and with full conviction. You know what kind of men we proved to be among you for your sake. And you became imitators of us and of the Lord, for you received the word in much affliction, with joy inspired by the Holy Spirit . . ." (1 Thes 1:5-6).

Echoing 1 Cor 15:19: "If it is for just this life that we have hoped in Christ, we are the most pitiable of all men"; Heb 13:14 affirms: "For here we have no lasting city, but we are seeking the one that is to come."

By keeping in mind this dynamic pilgrimage imagery of the Bible, we can more fluidly integrate an ongoing sensitivity and responsiveness to the word of God into our busy lives.

The word of God has always been on the run (cf. 2 Thes 3:1). It is dynamic, moving, evolving, and transforming. It can adapt itself to our lives if we reciprocate and accept the word on its own terms—which is one of the most difficult aspects of *lectio divina*, because it means giving up control and entrusting ourselves to God. This goes against everything our individualistic and materialistic culture condition us for.

This reciprocal, dialogical relationship with God's word is a fundamental dimension of *lectio divina* that is inclusive of not only the Bible, but all of life. It also underscores the honor and dignity conferred on human beings who alone of all creatures are privileged to engage God in conversation. From Eden forward, God has made Himself available to communicate with His children. He also desires our communication with each other, and the rest of creation, and in particular nature, which as the psalms proclaim reveal His glory. While He sets the parameters and determines the overall agenda of the dialogue, as illustrated throughout the Bible and the experience of the Church, He is also desirous of our input (cf. Lk 18:1-8).

*Lectio divina* is a timeless term descriptive of the intimate and ongoing interaction to which God invites us. The Bible is the manual and life is the laboratory. As in marriage, the biblical metaphor par excellence of our relationship with God, dialogue is at times frustrating, confusing, and painful. However, like the seed that falls to the ground, it eventually sprouts and brings life and joy if we continue watering it with our love. May we persevere in cooperating with Jesus, the sower, and act as faithful stewards.

In the next chapter, we will explore the nature of the word further, and the signs we receive along the way that help us achieve the growth that occurs secretly but surely in our journey to God's kingdom (cf. Mk 4:26-29).

# – Three –

## Word and Sacrament

IN this chapter we will consider the nature of the word and the  sacramental vision underlying it. All of life is a divine mystery that is revealed through signs and wonders that we often miss. It is interesting that John's Gospel, which elevates and illustrates the Word, is also the Gospel with the most pronounced sacramental outlook on life and that offers the concept of sign to illustrate the inauguration of God's kingdom by Jesus. The etymology of the word "Sacrament" includes the concepts of sign and mystery.

## What Is the Word?

Now that we are forewarned of what fidelity to the word entails, it is important to sharpen our understanding of what the word of God means from a theological, anthropological, and pastoral perspective. The concept of "word" is essential to an understanding of both the human and divine dimensions of the Bible.

The biblical concept of word (in Hebrew, *dabar*) was dynamic and multi-faceted. A word, and particularly God's, was not only an utterance, but a portent of meaning and action. The following verses illustrate this:

"Is not my word like fire, says the LORD, like a hammer shattering a rock?" (Jer 23:29).

"For just as the rain and the snow come down from the heavens and do not return there until they have watered the earth, making it fertile and fruitful, giving seed for the one who sows and bread for those who eat, so shall my word be that issues forth from my mouth. It will not return to me unfulfilled, but it will accomplish my purpose and achieve what I sent it forth to do" (Isa 55:10-11).

"All flesh is like grass, and all its glory like the flower of the field. The grass withers, and the flower fades, but the word of the Lord endures forever" (1 Pet 1:24-25; Isa 40:8).

"Indeed, the word of God is living and active. Sharper than any two-edged sword, it pierces to the point where it divides soul and spirit, joints and marrow; it judges the thoughts and the intentions of the heart" (Heb 4:12).

God's word is alive and efficacious. It demands a response. Being lukewarm is unacceptable (cf. Rev 3:15-16).

## Who Is the Word?

The Gospel and first letter of John used the Greek word *logos* ("word") to describe Jesus' pre-existence and pivotal role in creation (cf. Jn 1:1-18; 1 Jn 1:1-4). This language recalls the divine personification of wisdom in the Old Testament Wisdom books (cf. Prov 8:22-31; Sir 1:4-8; 24:9).

There is also a theological and literary connection between divine wisdom as presented in the Wisdom books and the Bread of Life discourse in John 6. The Eucharist, as anticipated in the Bread of Life discourse, was viewed by early Christians as Wisdom's banquet as prophesized in Prov 9:2-5, Sir 24:19-21, and Isa 55:1-3.

As observed in section 21 of *Dei Verbum*, the Mass reveals and celebrates the intrinsic link between word / wisdom and sacrament (particularly its penultimate expression, the Eucharist):

"The Church has always venerated the divine Scriptures just as she venerates the body of the Lord, since, especially in the sacred liturgy, she unceasingly receives and offers to the faithful the bread of life from the table both of God's word and of Christ's body."

- *When I attend Mass, do I recognize it as the fundamental context for* lectio divina, *in that it brings together Word, Sacrament, and community in thanksgiving to the Father?*

- *Do I respect and respond to these connections celebrated at Mass that we are to bring to daily life through love and truth?*

   *The Gospel of John seemingly illustrates this by omitting the words of consecration. The evangelist uses eucharistic language in the Bread of Life discourse (cf. Jn 6)—and narrates Jesus' feet-washing gesture at the Last Supper as a reminder of the attitude that must underlie commemoration of the Lord's Supper. Paul echoes this fraternal understanding in his account of the Eucharist (cf. 1 Cor 11:18-34).*

One of the interesting aspects of John's Gospel is that while it emphasizes Jesus' divinity more than the other Gospels, it also brings out Jesus' and other biblical characters' humanity in a profound and dramatic manner. Its earthiness as reflected in precise geographical and circumstantial details complements its lofty celestial horizons.

John presents Jesus as the meaning and force behind creation, the perfect communication and representation of God. In the words of Anglican biblical scholar John A.T. Robinson, He is the human face of God.

The Greek philosophers understood *logos* in a cosmic sense as the universal and divine wisdom, the meaning and reason for everything, the force behind the universe. A prominent Jewish philosopher, Philo of Alexandria (20 B.C.E.—50 C.E.), utilized the concept of *logos* to make Judaism comprehensible to a society immersed in Greek culture.

Parallels between Philo's and John's use of the term reveal that John was also bridging Hebrew / biblical and Greek / philosophical notions of word in describing Jesus and making Him comprehensible to a Hellenized (influenced by Greek culture) audience.

Such cultural accommodation occurs throughout the New Testament and Church history, but without compromising Christian values and doctrines. St. Paul drew upon Greek concepts of virtue (cf. Phil 4:8) in order to inspire his audience.

Pope Paul VI's concept of dialogue and *ostpolitik* (diplomatic initiatives designed to elicit concessions from the Soviets and their satellite nations rather than engage in confrontation) is an example of a contemporary adaptation that remains faithful to Catholic teachings. Pope John Paul's Theology of the Body teachings are an attempt to address modern society's preoccupation with sexuality with relevant Christian doctrines. Pope Benedict frequently emphasizes that Catholic teaching must be presented in a positive manner in the face of modern pessimism.

When we practice *lectio divina* cognizant of its inherent connections to life and God's ongoing providential initiative, we too will be able to link legitimate secular concepts with our faith. In this way we will be faithful to the call of Vatican II and the modern pontiffs to dialogue with and help build up the world by acknowledging and supporting its praiseworthy elements while sharing and practicing our faith without imposing it. A phrase often associated with this effort during the pontificate of John XXIII and Vatican Council II was "building up the human." St. Paul frequently used the term "building up" or an equivalent.

- *In what ways am I called to "build up the human"? What opportunities are available to me, and what steps can I take in response?*

## The Catholic Concept of God's Word

Catholicism recognizes other manifestations of God's word besides Jesus and the Bible. According to Genesis 1, all of creation and most importantly, human beings, proceeds from God's word. Nature and each person is a word/communication of God.

Because God's Spirit is in each person (cf. Gen 2:7), human beings are a more essential manifestation of God's word than nature. God identifies with each person (cf. Ex 3:7; Isa 58; Mt 25:31-46), particularly those who are suffering.

The Holy Spirit inspired the Bible for the purpose of enlightening and saving human beings. The letters and words in the

Bible of themselves are just an intermediary. It is what they communicate and represent, the intent and effect they have, that constitutes the essence of God's word. We should personalize and realize, rather than materialize and ideologize, God's word. Like the Sabbath, the Bible was created for man, and not man for the Bible (cf. Jn 1:1-18; Mk 2:27).

## The Word of God in Tradition and the Church

Catholics also believe that God's word is present in Tradition and in the faith of the contemporary community, both magisterial teaching and the *sensus fidelium* (the sense of the faithful). The Vatican II document on the Bible, *Dei Verbum*, teaches that Scripture and Tradition are not separate sources of revelation, but rather parallel streams from the same "divine wellspring."

Scripture began as oral tradition, so the two share the same essence and origin. Likewise the faith of the living Church as taught by the magisterium is not opposed to Scripture or Tradition, but rather safeguards, ponders (cf. Lk 2:19), and applies it to contemporary life.

All of this should convince us of the dynamic, omnipresent manifestations of God's word in our life. It also leads to the notion of divine and human signs, with which we shall close this chapter.

## Divine and Human Signs

When we practice *lectio divina*, we read a manageable portion of Scripture and proceed until we come upon a "word" that speaks to us. This can be a word, phrase, image, verse, or series of verses. It may also recall for us other "words" in the Bible or our life, using the dynamic notions of *dabar* and *logos* discussed earlier. Medieval monks referred to such mnemonic linking as reminiscence.

Christian tradition uses the phrase "divine signs" in a variety of ways, but with regards to *lectio divina* it refers to the word we receive during our pondering of Scripture, or the word that comes to us as God reveals Himself and His truth in life events. (It also refers to apparent manifestations of God's will and providence in life.)

For example, we find ourselves in the depths of discouragement and out of nowhere experience an inner consolation. Or someone reaches out to us with an example or message that we intuit could only have come from God. Because in this world God prefers to work through human instruments, many manifestations of divine providence have both a human and divine dimension. We are God's hands and feet. Whether a sign is of human or divine origin is less important than responding to it properly. Semantics is subordinate to efficacy and responsiveness.

The phrase "human signs" is akin to the "signs of the times" expression noted in Mt 16:3 and referenced in the Vatican II documents and frequently thereafter by Pope Paul VI. These are the events, circumstances, and developments in human experience that speak to us of important truths. The foreword to my book *Calming the Stormy Seas of Stress* contains an illuminative definition of the signs of the times by Pope Paul VI in an address on April 16, 1969.

We typically don't refer to these as divine because at least on the surface they come primarily from human experience rather than divine intervention, though of course given the mysterious omnipresence of divine providence, there is no hard and fast distinction. Divine signs give us a more direct and distinct impression of divine initiative or providence. Of course, only the Holy Spirit can infallibly discern the difference.

## Distinctions

As mentioned, the distinctions between divine and human signs are not as important as the impetus we give to them. Recognizing such signs is an affirmation of God's ongoing involvement in our lives and humanity's essential orientation towards the divine. It gives practical expression to a central tenet of the faith: Jesus lives. We have the freedom to reject Him, but we cannot escape Him.

The word "Sacrament" means "sacred sign," and thus we can view these human and divine signs as prompts, pointers, and reminders. *Lectio divina* also has a sacramental dimension, both in terms of the divine and human signs that it engages and the biblical basis of the Sacraments, which are also amenable to the activities that constitute *lectio divina*.

## Discernment

Through discernment aided by the Holy Spirit and in dialogue with the Church, we are able to recognize divine signs. We must submit our discernment to the Church's judgment through frequent confession, spiritual direction, consultation of magisterial teaching, and conscience examination. Like the biblical characters, we are susceptible to misjudgment and prejudices. God helps us cope with and correct them, but we are never entirely free of them in this life.

As you become more comfortable with *lectio divina* and progress in the spiritual life, you'll develop a more refined intuition and sensitivity to divine signs. Correspondingly, the more you learn about yourself, human nature, and life, the more perceptive and responsive you will be to human signs. Nature and grace cooperate to help us maintain divine and human signs in a healthy tension.

## Humility

Of course, it is imperative that we be modest and humble in our assessments, and not impose them upon others. I may believe that God is speaking to me in a certain way through the Bible, creation, human events, magisterial teaching, or the Sacraments, but that does not mean that my interpretation and application is correct. Accordingly, it is best to let the awareness and identification of divine signs come to us in the Spirit's own time. As discussed in the final chapter, we want to avoid the trap of an excessively, and unconsciously self-serving, mystical approach to life. Beware the self-anointed prophet.

Christianity is an incarnational religion, and Jesus and the Church embrace all that is truly human, so we should have our hands full dealing with human realities without artificially injecting divine connotations. God's initiative, divine providence, or signs, can't be forced or manipulated.

Just as contemplation and consolation are divine gifts, so discernment of divine mysteries is a grace bestowed through God's initiative. The saints who received divine disclosures did so humbly and for the benefit of the Church. Exploitation of these privileged revelations was unthinkable for them, and should be for us as well, in whatever way and degree that God speaks to us.

Fulfilling our human duties and responsibilities inherently entails a fidelity to the divine will, so we are better off dispensing with excessive religious rhetoric (what I like to call "God talk"), and instead focus on living it, which will undoubtedly tap all our energies.

To perceive divine or human signs, I must be listening and receptive. If I don't believe that God is active in the world and in my life, I am unlikely to perceive or receive miraculous divine persuasion. As illustrated in 1 Kings 19:1-13, God typically speaks through "the still small voice," the sound of silence, the almost imperceptible movement of the Spirit, the natural course of human events, activities, and interactions, or natural phenomena—in the Bible, these include earthquakes, thunder, strong winds, and fire, which the pagans often deified—rather than through miraculous interventions.

How do I recognize the signs of the times and of my life? Again, by listening and awareness, a heart open to God and our brothers and sisters. Sometimes others (e.g., friends, family, a spiritual director or confessor) observe what we are blind to. Hopefully we communicate a humble openness that invites their candor. *Lectio divina* sharpens our antennae and fine-tunes our reception. As discussed, the concepts of divine and human signs are not entirely distinct, for certainly when we recognize human signs there is a divine inspiration and capacity that enables us to do so. Who can rule out God's participation in the particular human events or circumstances which we attach significance to? Who can know the mind of God? (cf. Isa 40:13-14; 55:8-9; Rom 11:33-35).

As mentioned, it is mistaken and counterproductive to strain to recognize divine and human signs, or to force interpretations of them. They'll come on their own, and as we grow spiritually and humanly, we will increasingly be able to recognize them and respond appropriately.

Personally, I don't discuss these signs with anyone but my spiritual director and confidants because frankly I am not sure that my discernment is correct. Ultimately, the terminology we assign to these events or markers is less important than the attitude with which we respond to them. My discernment of such signs is personal and subjective and is in no way universal and definitive. The key is to maintain an ongoing dialogue with God, neighbor, and the Church. This will help clarify things for us, though we still must walk by faith rather than by sight (cf. 2 Cor 5:7).

- *Am I attentive to the providential prompts that I receive? How might I be more responsive and cooperative?*

## Discernment Resources

Within Catholic tradition, numerous strains of spirituality have contributed to our understanding of discernment. Among the most influential spiritualities would be the Franciscan, Carmelite, and Ignatian, though arguments could be made for the inclusion of others.

Franciscan discernment principles reflect the charisms of Francis of Assisi and their Order and are generally sensate-sensitive and creation-oriented. We discover God in the world, not in the pantheistic manner of the pagans, but with reference to God's creative activity and ongoing providence. Carmelite principles are primarily based on the teachings of St. Teresa of Avila and St. John of the Cross. St. Ignatius instituted a whole series of guidelines and principles for discernment, the Spiritual Exercises, and in particular the Rules for the Discernment of Spirits, that have stood the test of time.

The classic popular treatment of Carmelite and Ignatian discernment principles is Fr. Thomas Green, S.J.'s *Weeds Among the Wheat: Discernment: Where Prayer and Action Meet.* Mary and Joseph are the supreme examples in Christian tradition of discernment as Fr. Green defines it in his subtitle.

## The Significance of Signs

Going back to John's Gospel, which uses the term "signs" instead of miracles, the concept of signs has been very important in Christian spirituality and doctrine. One of the chief ways God makes Himself known is through signs, that is, events or entities that reveal His presence and message.

Becoming sensitive to divine and human signs is fundamental to biblical and Catholic spirituality. One of the fundamental teachings of the Bible and Catholicism is the divine initiative. Beginning with Adam and Eve, continuing in a new phase with Abraham and Moses, and culminating in Jesus, God has been revealing Himself and acting in human history. Normative revelation ended with the Bible, but God continues to speak and act. His outreach and our cooperation has both an individual and communal component. This is a fundamental reason why our practice of *lectio divina* should have both a personal and communal dimension.

## Journaling with Signs

When I journal at the end of the day, I close my entry with my response to the question: How was God in my life today? In other words, what divine and human signs did I perceive, or lack thereof, and how did I respond?

Much of my preceding journal entry is composed of my discernment, recounting, and analysis of human signs, and their significance and lessons. I am cautious about ascribing to God what belongs to man, even though providence underlies all human affairs. Though my answer to this question may mostly deal with human signs, such distinctions are not essential to the underlying issue of the divine initiative and my response. Thus journaling becomes a tool for integrating divine and human signs and making them more concrete by getting them on paper and assessing my responsiveness. In the next chapter, you will encounter a model within both Judaism and Christianity for discerning and journaling on the divine initiative.

## Signs Summary

Recognizing and responding to divine and human signs is an imperfect science. Since these signs could also be understood as "words" in the biblical sense discussed above, our reaction is susceptible to all the contingencies associated with *lectio divina* and biblical interpretation and spirituality in general. However, it is in coping with and persevering amid such obstacles that we grow closer to Jesus, Mary, and Joseph, who knew such difficulties more intimately than we.

And since, as discussed throughout this book, the process of *lectio divina* is analogous to the marital relationship, with both designed to be a dynamic dialogue, the closeness that we gain is our greatest end and reward; hence, the overall theme of the united Holy Family as a model of *lectio divina*.

The confusion and subsequent exchange between Jesus and His parents when they found Him in the temple (cf. Lk 2:41-52) assures us, along with various papal and traditional teachings on the subject, that Mary and Joseph were not exempt from human ignorance, misunderstandings, and conflicts. Their obedience to God's word and each other, in the process of wrestling with these challenges, constitutes the greatest examples of *lectio divina* in history. The annunciations to Joseph and Mary, and subsequent events recorded within the Bible in reference to them, offer us not only source material for *lectio*, but a model in itself. Such is the power of grace and virtue.

May the Holy Family continue to inspire and assist us as we walk in their footsteps.

In the next chapter we will explore the dialogical foundations and connotations of *lectio divina*, followed by a reflection on the dialogical dispositions of the genders in the context of the Holy Family and their practice of *lectio divina*. Chapters on Mary and then Joseph as models of *lectio divina* will follow and conclude the book.

# – Four –

## The *Lectio Divina* Dialogue

"PAUL VI had a marked capacity for friendship, a surprising respect for whomever spoke to him, a rare ability to show that two were needed in a dialogue, not just one. He made one feel, truly and unpretentiously, that whomever he was speaking to was important to him and from that person he mysteriously expected something decisive. He was ready to give very generously but without ever making his giving a burden. Indeed he seemed to be excusing himself for it, asking that it be seen as something obvious, so that the real, personal aspect of the relationship might not change.

"For this reason he did not see dialogue merely as an instrument but as a method reflecting the dialogical makeup of his personality. And so, without being compelled to say so, he felt close to modern people, close also to those who were distant or who opposed him in theory or in practice. This is why his pontificate, moving rapidly forward in the way prophetically indicated by Pope John XXIII, was to provide for the Church an audience and a worldwide respect in which the charism of mass encounters with people, characteristic of Pope John Paul II, could be freely prepared.

". . . As the passing of time moves us further and further from the earthly existence of Paul VI, his spiritual figure comes closer to us. More and more we understand that he was truly one of us, a man of our age who freed us from the danger of shutting ourselves up in our age, who helped us dialogue with the past, who gave us the courage and the joy to become contemporaries of Christ," (*Journeying with the Lord*, Cardinal Carlo Maria Martini).

The dialogical disposition evoked during *lectio divina* should transfer to our lives. Paul VI was a living example of this. The consummating stage of action includes this continuation of responsiveness to the word we receive in *lectio*. Of course, we need not limit ourselves to just one word or the word we experienced during *lectio*. As *lectio* is a Spirit-driven practice, we should not place rigid and artificial limits on the divine initiative.

Just as there are multiple ways of communicating, likewise there is no one way to practice *lectio*. Persons with a contemplative disposition, particularly members of religious orders with that charism and lifestyle, will typically be drawn to focus on one word and use it as an entrée to contemplation. Others with an apostolic vocation and active lifestyle and an intellectual or analytical orientation may experience inspiration from multiple words. Each person and *lectio* experience is unique. While respecting the guidelines and traditional structure of *lectio*, you should feel free to respond reflexively to the flow and directives of the Spirit. With familiarity with *lectio*, you will develop a rhythm, confidence, and comfort level that will enable you to discern how to proceed.

## Situational Dialogue

One of the ways in which we tie the rhythm of our life to that of Scripture is by identifying intensely with a character or circumstance in Scripture. This is particularly efficacious during difficult times in which psychological and practical remedies are lacking, and we are thrown into a radical dependence on divine providence and mercy as well as our own resourcefulness and perseverance.

I often refer to this as the prophetic dimension of *lectio* in the sense that we find ourselves engaged in the dialogue of salvation in the footsteps of believers who have gone before us. Usually this involves suffering and a witness to God's love and truth, which thereby makes it prophetic. God uses us to speak to others and the world, even if it is to only one person.

One obvious example is couples who are unable to have a child. Their infertility assumes a prophetic dimension in the sense that they follow in the footsteps of the numerous biblical couples who had difficulty conceiving, but whose plight became part of God's salvific plan. These couples witness to their love and fidelity to each other and God when they remain faithful despite the apparent fruitlessness of their procreative efforts. Reflections in the *lectio divina* format are found in my book *Bearing the Unbearable: Coping with Infertility and Other Profound Suffering*.

*Lectio* and life are so closely connected that our attentiveness to the dialogue of salvation, and our need to dialogue with God and others, naturally and supernaturally (through the inspiration of the Spirit) brings us closer to God's word. We resonate with the biblical text and characters and the challenges they faced. The more we interact with Scripture, the more we realize our connectedness to the communion of saints, those who have gone before (cf. Heb 11:1—12:1).

Reading the signs of the times and our lives in dialogue with Scripture alerts us to connections and parallels that help us cope with the challenges in our life that elude earthly remedies.

For example, the person whose spouse is unfaithful or has abandoned them, but who refuses to retaliate and chooses forgiveness instead, can relate to Hosea, in particular the first three chapters. So many feelings rush to consciousness that even a person with good intentions can be overwhelmed. Dialoging with God through Hosea enables us to bring ourselves and our circumstances to God on a holistic level, including unconscious dimensions that need healing. In reading Hosea, we discover parallels with our experience that become springboards to dialogue.

Heartbreaking, conflictual experiences can get us on an analytical merry-go-round. *Lectio divina* gets us off this cycle by having us rest and trust in God and open ourselves to His will for our life. We take the focus off of ourselves and our problems and onto God's perspective through His word and the influence of the Holy Spirit.

Sometimes the dialogue that evolves is a wordless one. It becomes a meeting of hearts and wills. We just want to be there with God and perhaps others. In chapter one, we referred to this as simple presence. Words are insufficient to express the intimacy we experience.

The person who is divorced against their will can turn to the exchange between Jesus and His Apostles shortly after Jesus' response to the Pharisees about the conditions for divorce. Peter voiced the amazement of the Apostles at Jesus' prohibition of remarriage after divorce. Shortly thereafter Jesus discusses celibacy for the sake of God's kingdom, which while generally interpreted to refer to those who voluntarily give up sexual relations can also be applied to abandoned spouses who choose to remain single out of respect for the indissolubility of marriage. Recognizing that the Apostles were practically scandalized by Jesus' strict moral code with regards to divorce can inspire us to be brutally honest with God as we struggle with this teaching and God's will for us.

So many timeless situations are anticipated in the Bible. The person who loses a spouse can identify with Ezekiel (cf. Ezek 24:15-18), who responds in restrained, Job-like fashion to the sudden death of his wife (cf. Job 1—2) at the command of the Lord. Scripture's silence as to his inner thoughts and emotions is an invitation to join our thoughts and circumstances to his in an intimate dialogue with the Lord and perhaps Ezekiel or other saints as well.

The concise, poignant wording of Scripture (e.g., Ezekiel is told that by a sudden blow God is taking away "the delight of your eyes") helps us get to the core of issues and enter deeply into our suffering in such a way that we allow it to become meaningful, transformational, and redemptive, a precursor to joy.

Jeremiah's involuntary celibacy (cf. Jer 16:1-4) can be a source of consolation for single persons unable to find a partner. Instead of viewing themselves as rejected or inadequate, they can recognize that God has other plans for them. In the Old Testament, single life was shunned and looked upon as an inferior state. The person was incomplete, unfulfilled. Reading the aforementioned verses from Jeremiah as well as other passages from the book where he complains to God can deepen our identification with the prophet and help us recognize both that our involuntary vocation is part of God's plan and that He understands our need to voice our displeasure. *Lectio divina* is one context for this dialogue.

Identifying with biblical characters in no way makes a situation easier or painless. Rather, we engage our difficulty on the proper level, the moral or spiritual dimension, where we have God's consolation, mercy, and wisdom to rely on. We gradually discover that our narrow perspective is not all there is, and that by remaining open to God's plan while accepting the brokenness in ourselves and others we participate constructively in His redemptive plan.

In his encyclical on Christian suffering, *Salvifici Doloris*, Pope John Paul points out that some suffering is beyond the reach of psychotherapy. What the pope refers to as moral suffering includes not only relational difficulties, such as infidelity, abandonment, loss, alienation, and loneliness, but any affliction of the heart. Such can only be adequately healed and transformed by God. *Lectio* is a forum for participating in the dialogue of salvation that enables our hearts to be softened and placed at God's disposal (cf. Jer 31:31-34).

Deep wounds are rarely healed all at once. The scars remain, and we must continually return to God and the Church for healing and rehabilitation. *Lectio* can be a helpful practice in this regard. Passages such as the aforementioned, and others we resonate with, can become venues for facing rather than running away from our suffering and thereby joining Jesus in His (which is the ultimate vocation of His disciples).

Whenever I find myself overly analytical and unable to resolve intense emotions and disappointments, I turn to

Scripture and enter into a dialogue with the Lord. This helps me to regain my bearings, take up my cross again, and gain perspective. The Bible consistently acknowledges the challenges and difficulties faced by believers. It is good to be reminded of such so that we don't reflexively view our suffering as an indictment. The Beatitudes are a handy, *lectio*-accessible, reminder that the best is yet to come.

*What biblical characters and texts do I most relate to? Why?*

*What role does the Bible play in my life during difficult times?*

*What parallels or connections can I identify with my life?*

## The Three Stages in the Life of Moses

Of all the Old Testament historical characters, perhaps Moses was most intimately acquainted with deep suffering. Despite all his efforts, he was denied entrance into the Promised Land. The abundance of biblical texts dealing with Moses facilitate our dialogue with him.

A helpful model that is complementary to *lectio* is known as the three stages in the life of Moses. It is based on Acts 7:17-43, St. Stephen's speech shortly before his martyrdom. A Jewish midrash states that three famous rabbis, Hillel the Elder, Jonathan ben Zakkai, and Akiva ben Joseph, along with Moses, lived to be 120 years old. Hillel was a contemporary of Jesus, ben Zakkai was pivotal in the survival of Judaism after the destruction of the temple in 70 C.E., and Akiva was burned at the stake by the Romans in 135 C.E. in response to the Bar Kokhba uprising. Akiva believed Bar Kokhba was the messiah.

In St. Stephen's speech, Moses' life is divided into three forty-year periods that can be categorized as follows:

1) Acquiring methods (education and formation)—Moses' time in Egypt during which he was brought up in the house of Pharaoh and received a privileged education in the Egyptian schools.

2) Generosity and failure—Moses' time in the desert after he is forced to flee Egypt in response to his slaying of the Egyptian taskmaster.

3) Discovery of the divine initiative—Moses' encounter with God at the burning bush, and his subsequent interactions with God in the process of leading Israel out of Egypt and to the brink of the Promised Land.

The terminology for these stages is borrowed from Cardinal Carlo Martini, S.J., as articulated in his modern spiritual classic *Through Moses to Jesus.* Extensive excerpts and a detailed discussion of these stages are found in my book *Journaling with Moses and Job.*

This is an accessible and pliable personal and spiritual development model that is well-suited to the challenge of *lectio* and Christian living, as follows.

## Acquiring Methods

The first part of *lectio* is becoming familiar with the process, learning how to do it. This corresponds to the stage of acquiring methods. We learn the structure, components, and guidelines for practicing it effectively. Here we are primarily at the level of theory and concept. We learn how things are supposed to work, and what to do when they don't.

At this point it is not too difficult to retain our idealism. We are enthusiastic about the new process and the prospects of discoveries and growth. The principles and practices we learn seem credible, and when we try them in a controlled environment (e.g., a Bible-sharing group or retreat weekend) they seem to work. We feel good about God and ourselves and the Church because this model we are getting acquainted with seems to add something to our life, and to bring us closer to God, ourselves, and others. So far, so good, but there's more.

## Generosity and Failure

There is typically a honeymoon period in any spiritual endeavor or stage, just as in marriage or other relational, productive, or developmental endeavors. While we are in the stage we don't anticipate the honeymoon ending because we are experiencing too much fulfillment. We don't conceive of how or why it could end, because we are simply applying what we have learned.

We all know honeymoons don't last, and the same is true in the spiritual life. As we practice *lectio*, we eventually encounter unanticipated difficulties for which we do not have ready solutions. The answers aren't in the textbook, nor are they easily discovered through reflection and reading. We have to work through them in dialogue with the Church, and wait upon God, but He and the solution seem to be a long time in coming.

This is the stage of reality in which the tidy theories and practices we learned in the first stage are found to be inadequate for the challenges of *lectio* in real world circumstances. For example, we find ourselves falling asleep during *lectio*, so we resolve to get more sleep at night and not eat immediately before *lectio*, when our digestion tends to disrupt our *lectio* and our body rhythms make us sleepy.

Despite our intentions, we periodically find ourselves following food with *lectio*, and end up feeling bloated or nodding off. Whenever we do succeed in separating our nutritional and spiritual nourishment, we still occasionally experience grogginess and end up dozing off, sometimes because we are anxious or tired, other times because we are relaxed. In any event, we can't seem to consistently coordinate our physical and spiritual schedules in a way conducive to fulfilling *lectio*. Even when we make the necessary schedule adjustments, we don't reap the fruits according to our expectations.

Or we plan our day to allow sufficient quiet time, but unforeseen events occur that disrupt our rhythm and schedule. Whenever we are successful in carving out the time and engaging in *lectio*, we experience dryness and distance from God. The word doesn't speak to us, and we feel empty and discouraged. Why engage in a dialogue with a silent and unresponsive partner? Or, when we're the unresponsive and disinterested one, why make the effort? Such negativity and laxness brings us and others down. Hope is the answer. Pope Benedict XVI recognized this need in modern life and wrote the profound encyclical *Spe Salvi* on it.

At times it seems like no matter what we do, our progress is sporadic and far less than we hoped for. Efforts don't yield results in the anticipated manner, and our generosity seems to lead to failure. Good intentions don't always bear fruit, and it often seems as if we receive the opposite of what we should.

I experience this occasionally in writing on *lectio*. I come up with good ideas, at least from my perspective, put them into a file, and then the computer crashes and all is lost. I ask myself, why bother? Why does the timing have to be so bad?

Many people who attend Bible-sharing groups that I lead comment on how frustrated they get reading and trying to understand Scripture. They may not be following the *lectio* model per se, but they are trying to read the Bible and find it not only cryptic, but at times disconcerting. They are tempted to give up the practice entirely.

The correspondence between efforts and results just isn't there to our satisfaction, and we find our endeavors fruitless. We seem to be at a dead end, at least for the moment.

## Discovery of the Divine Initiative

Next is the consummating and most important stage of our model, our discovery of the divine initiative. We might also call this divine signs, because we experience providence in an explicit fashion that we feel must be more than mere coincidence.

Within *lectio*, we find the words of Scripture speaking to us in a new and revitalizing way. The Bible comes alive, and not necessarily because of anything that we have done. Even factoring in our efforts, something more seems to be happening. God seems to come out of hiding, and things no longer seem as if they all depend on us. The dryness and darkness become the spring that Pope Benedict has spoken of. The divine gardener seems to be watering our efforts, and we discern God speaking and reaching out to us.

Of course, eventually we experience periods of dryness and darkness again, and we go back into the Mosaic cycle. We never completely escape any of the stages because there is always more to learn, overcome, and integrate. The three stages are dynamic and fluid in the sense of repeating themselves according to the dictates of the Spirit and the vicissitudes of life. Our *lectio* time gradually assumes the Mosaic pattern of learning, stumbling, and being rescued, and we become more comfortable with the rhythm and how to respond to it. Of course, it never becomes static or easy, and we are always challenged to discern the human and divine signs that shed light on the Scriptures and our experience and disposition, and offer us hope and direction.

## Dialogue and Confession

One of the interesting sacramental applications of the dialogical dimension of *lectio divina* involves the Sacrament of Reconciliation. The most neglected Sacrament since Vatican Council II is Confession. This is ironic and unfortunate because it has been reformed into a more personal experience of God's mercy and the Church's compassion.

The 1983 Synod addressed the Sacrament, and in 1984 John Paul II issued the Apostolic Exhortation *Reconciliatio et Paenitentia* ("Reconciliation and Penance"), and in 2002 the *Motu Proprio* ("on his own impulse") *Misericordia Dei* ("The Mercy of God"). In both documents John Paul II explicitly referred to the Sacrament as being in a state of crisis. The following *lectio*-based, dialogical model of Confession is one way to revitalize our experience of the Sacrament.

## The Human Context of Reconciliation

First we must address the practical and pastoral considerations. Many persons shy away from Confession because of negative experiences with confessors or because they feel they can go directly to God for forgiveness. The presence of the Holy Spirit does not make either the confessor or penitent immune to human weakness. On a human level, we can have both good and bad experiences in Confession. We have to be mature enough to move beyond any negative experiences and focus on the sacramental graces of contrition, forgiveness, reform, and renewal.

At the Last Supper (cf. Lk 22:31-32), Jesus invites Peter to exercise the ministry of reconciliation, a vocation also recognized by Paul (cf. 2 Cor 5:18) and passed on to us. The Church has never taught that Confession is the sole vehicle of divine pardon and reconciliation. However, at times it is necessary on several levels: theological, moral, pastoral, psychological, and spiritual. Humans are interdependent and Christianity is a community religion. There are occasions where we need human confirmation of God's forgiveness, and the prudent counsel of an objective and compassionate listener. Because our sins harm our relationship with the body of Christ, the confessor, in a representative way, welcomes us back. We are not always able to reconcile directly with others.

Confession also works in the other direction. If you feel harmed by a priest or another member of the body of Christ, bring your pain into Confession. We need to forgive others along with being forgiven. The Sacrament of Reconciliation is a suitable forum for petitioning the grace to forgive and heal.

## Practical Suggestions for Confessor and Penitent

The new rite of Reconciliation invites us to begin with a brief reading from Scripture, usually a psalm, selected by the confessor. This recalls the reading stage of *lectio*. Then after sharing how long it has been since our previous Confession, we begin with a confession of praise, i.e., thanking God. This begins our encounter on a positive note and is in keeping with the fundamental human activity of praising God.

Theologically this is very sound, as indicated in the Lord's Prayer, which begins with a petition that God's name will be revered. We focus first on God, then on us. This positive beginning helps us to see our failings in a balanced manner and in a redemptive, hopeful light while emphasizing God's mercy and providence.

The next step is the confession of life, the emptying of our sins and burdens onto God's lap. "Come to me, all you who labor and are burdened, and I will give you rest" (Mt 11:28). We disclose to the priest the particular sins for which we are sorry, and the matters that are weighing on us and disturbing our peace. We share our burden with the Church and entrust it to the Lord.

The final step is to engage in a confession of faith, to express our trust in divine healing and forgiveness. This is given formal expression in our act of contrition, but we can also inject our own thoughts and resolutions either prior to or as part of the act of contrition. When the confessor suggests "make an act of contrition," we can use the framework of the prayer while putting our contrition in our own words as part of the reconciliatory dialogue. Confession thereby becomes a sacramental expression of the dialogue of salvation.

- *How do I view the Sacrament of Reconciliation? Do I* **celebrate** *it?*
- *If applicable, what is holding me back from more frequent Confession? How might I address any obstacles?*

## Dialogue in the Church

When Jesus conferred the power to forgive sins, He did so in the context of sharing His *shalom* (peaceful sense of well-being). To experience this *shalom* I need to reconcile myself with God and my brothers and sisters both directly and through the ministry of the Church. *Lectio divina* contributes to this process by its facilitation of a dialogical attitude towards God, His word and Church, and our neighbor. Dialogue is much different than inquisition, moralizing imperatives, static formulas, or empty words.

In fact, dialogue was the dynamic theme of Vatican II, beginning with Pope John XXIII's desire to open the windows of the Church and Paul VI's promotion of dialogue as the appropriate disposition and mode through which to conduct communications within and outside the Church. This dialogical disposition was affirmed in considerable detail in John Paul II's first encyclical *Redemptor Hominis* ("Redeemer of Man"), and by his actions throughout his pontificate. His non-violent, dialogical approach to Poland and the Soviet Union was pivotal in obtaining religious freedom and bringing down the Soviet Union. Benedict XVI has likewise been dialogical, charting a middle course for the Church and encouraging a more positive presentation of the faith.

Awareness, Renewal, and Dialogue were the three primary themes of Paul's first encyclical *Ecclesiam Suam*, and they are also three lynchpins of the *lectio divina* approach to spirituality and life proposed in this book.

They bear reflection and assimilation in our attempt to emulate Mary and Joseph in being faithful to God's word.

## Awareness

Pope Paul VI wanted the Church to take a good look at herself and the world around her. He wanted us to read and respond prudently to the signs of the times. Forty-five years later, an objective assessment of the Church's discernment and response is about what we could expect of a human institution, even one with a divine commission and presence. Some signs we read and responded to properly, others we misread, still others we missed entirely. Hence the confusion and disillusionment, as well as exhilaration and renewal, that followed Vatican II. Progress and reform ensued slowly and sporadically.

Our sign-reading mission remains. This includes reading the signs of our lives, the initiatives God is taking in our life and the message He is imparting, often through others and the Church. This is an aspect of self-awareness that Paul VI was encouraging. We need to continually ask ourselves, and perhaps reflect or journal on, the following:

- *What are the main signs of the times, both positive and negative? What are the signs of my life, i.e., the fundamental values and challenges facing me? How will I deal with them?*

*Lectio divina* is ideally equipped to foster such sign-reading, which in theological language is referred to as discernment—listening to the Spirit as we seek to discover the significance and meaning of the events in our lives, the Church, and the world around us.

Awareness is particularly important for laypersons who practice *lectio divina* on the run, fitting it in among their many responsibilities. The beautiful quote about maternity in 1 Tim 2:15: "However, women will be saved through the bearing of children, provided that they continue to persevere in faith, love, and holiness, marked by modesty," reminds us that living our vocation faithfully is pleasing to God, and that we should not draw a sharp distinction between our apostolic and devotional life.

## Renewal

Renewal reminds us that the Church is always reforming *Semper Reformanda*. We never arrive. Let he who stands take heed lest he fall (cf. 1 Cor 10:12).

*Lectio* never ceases to offer new wrinkles that remind us of the dynamism of Christian faith and our vocation. As befitting the Bible, its source material, *lectio* continually shows us something new (cf. Isa 43:18-19; Rev 21:5).

## Author's Experience

In fact, as I was doing my *lectio* last evening, I discovered another nuance in my practice. I went to *lectio* after dinner and fell asleep after making little progress. I didn't think I was tired, but apparently I was. I read a few lines from one of my previous books and I was out. (Stimulating reading.) I was also not in a great mood, so I was mostly doing *lectio* out of habit and a sense of duty—I put in the time and see what happens. I was feeling dry and empty, and not particularly hopeful of being nourished by the word at that moment.

After waking up I took a break and watched an old TV series rerun. I kept this diversion short, and then gradually began to feel "on," that is, disposed to the word. I could feel the Spirit moving and my own receptivity to the word increasing.

So I tried again, more than an hour after my first effort, and I found my intuitions to be on target. I'm hitting on all cylinders, in tune with the word. I immerse myself in the Sunday readings, and immediately see the salient themes—in this case, conversion and repentance. So I go with the *lectio* flow and keep my practice simple, avoiding any unnecessary analysis or intellectualizing or emotionalizing. I ask myself the simple question so typical of *lectio*: Am I willing to be converted, to continue the renewal process? In terms of a practical response, the action stage of *lectio*, what small steps or attitude changes might this entail? In the spirit of Psalm 130, I don't set my expectations too high, but simply listen and follow the Spirit's lead, as best I can discern.

## Dialogue

Of course, I had no Angel whispering in my ear, appearing to me, or speaking to me in a dream. And I certainly didn't feel a spiritual high or ecstasy. Just a sense of peace, like a spouse feeling comfortable with their partner after they break through the dryness and renew the dialogue. The word I received of the need for ongoing conversion remains with me, a spiritual wake-up call. It reminds me to get back to basics and pay attention to the signs God has put in my path, prompts to change, grow, heal, and reach out. A dynamic dialogue initiated by God, narrated throughout the Bible, and continuing in history and in the Church. An open, forgiving, reconciling, dialogical disposition towards others is a fulfillment of the Lord's commandment. Thus *lectio* helps us fulfill the two great commandments with our whole selves.

- *Am I willing to respond to God's invitation for an ongoing dialogue about His will for my life, recalling the obedience of Mary and Joseph in simple, hidden ways?*

- *Am I willing to engage others in constructive conversation, listening to and observing them, not to judge, but to support and affirm?*

Dialogue can assume many forms and contexts: transcendent, familial, social, interior, professional, pastoral, ecumenical, and evangelical.

Dialogue, the underlying theme of Pope Paul's first encyclical *Ecclesiam Suam* ("Paths of the Church"), and his last major document, the December 8, 1975 Apostolic Exhortation *Evangelii Nuntiandi* ("On Evangelization in the Modern World"), and indeed his entire pontificate, has been omnipresent in this book and highlighted in this chapter. But the conversation is just beginning.

## Christian Communication Principles

In sections 80-83 of *Ecclesiam Suam*, Paul VI articulates the dialogical disposition that should underlie our *lectio* lifestyle. God's word is dynamic and should affect all aspects of our life and relationships. Like a spouse, God wants our all.

80. Hence, the dialogue supposes that we possess a state of mind which we intend to communicate to others and to foster in all our neighbors: It is a state of mind of one who feels within himself the burden of the apostolic mandate, of one who realizes that he can no longer separate his own salvation from the endeavor to save others, of one who strives constantly to put the message of which he is custodian into the mainstream of human discourse.

81. The dialogue is, then, a method of accomplishing the apostolic mission. It is an example of the art of spiritual communication. Its characteristics are the following:

(1) Clearness above all; the dialogue supposes and demands comprehensibility. It is an outpouring of thought; it is an invitation to the exercise of the highest powers which man possesses. This very claim would be enough to classify the dialogue among the best manifestations of human activity and culture. This fundamental requirement is enough to enlist our apostolic care to review every angle of our language to guarantee that it be understandable, acceptable, and well-chosen.

(2) A second characteristic of the dialogue is its meekness, the virtue which Christ sets before us to be learned from Him: "Learn of me, because I am meek and humble of heart" (cf. Mt 11:29). The dialogue is not proud, it is not bitter, it is not offensive. Its authority is intrinsic to the truth it explains, to the charity it communicates, to the example it proposes; it is not a command, it is not an imposition. It is peaceful; it avoids violent methods; it is patient; it is generous.

(3) Trust, not only in the power of one's words, but also in an attitude of welcoming the trust of the interlocutor. Trust promotes confidence and friendship. It binds hearts in mutual adherence to the good which excludes all self-seeking.

(4) Finally, pedagogical prudence, which esteems highly the psychological and moral circumstances of the listener, (cf. Mt 7:6) whether he be a child, uneducated, unprepared, diffident, hostile. Prudence strives to learn the sensitivities of the hearer and requires that we adapt ourselves and the manner of our presentation in a reasonable way lest we be displeasing and incomprehensible to him.

82. In the dialogue, conducted in this manner, the union of truth and charity, of understanding and love is achieved.

83. In the dialogue one discovers how different are the ways which lead to the light of faith, and how it is possible to make them converge on the same goal. Even if these ways are divergent, they can become complementary by forcing our reasoning process out of the worn paths and by obliging it to deepen its research, to find fresh expressions.

The dialectic of this exercise of thought and of patience will make us discover elements of truth also in the opinions of others, it will force us to express our teaching with great fairness, and it will reward us for the work of having explained it in accordance with the objections of another or despite his slow assimilation of our teaching. The dialogue will make us wise; it will make us teachers.

## The Modern Popes, Vatican II, and *Lectio Divina*

I strongly encourage you to read the aforementioned documents along with John Paul II's first (March 4, 1979) encyclical, *Redemptor Hominis* ("Redeemer of Man"), by which he set a tone and direction for his papacy and continued the implementation of Vatican II.

Practicing *lectio* on these documents can provide three critical benefits:

First, you will learn the importance of communication, particularly but not exclusively from a spiritual and moral perspective, within a familial and pastoral setting. The Bible records no dialogue between Jesus' parents but narrates their disposition and activities in profound brevity so that we can fill in the blanks through reflection, prayer, and emulation. Reflection on *Ecclesiam Suam, Redemptor Hominis,* and the biblical texts on the Holy Family can help you develop a dialogical disposition at home, church (parish life), and in secular settings.

Second, you will take up the challenge posed by Paul VI in *Evangelii Nuntiandi* to continually be evangelized and then share the good news in word and primarily deed and example. Pope Paul offers such splendid and comprehensive guidance that none of the subsequent popes have issued a major document on evangelization. When they teach on the subject, they mainly reference *Evangelii Nuntiandi.* Jesus and the Church need witnesses in a world that has increasingly lost its way. *Lectio divina* is not meant to be privatized. The word is meant to be lived and shared.

Third, *Redemptor Hominis* shows the continuity between John XXIII, Paul VI, Vatican II, and John Paul II that is often overlooked today due to the rise of polarizing ideologies that are incompatible with the Gospel. John Paul II practiced dialogue in his own way, just as the other modern popes have. Each reflects their ethnic, cultural, academic, and ecclesiastical background. John XXIII brings a historical perspective, Paul VI a diplomatic, psychological, sociological, and aesthetic perspective, John Paul I a pastoral perspective, John Paul II an anthropological, philosophical, and political perspective, and Benedict a theological perspective, though of course there is much overlap. We should consult the writings and examples of each of these popes (without excluding prior ones, of course) in order to broaden, balance, and enrich our practice of *lectio divina.*

So much of what the modern popes teach and represent is misinterpreted and distorted both by the media and ideologues at both extremes, and much of this trickles down to the grassroots level. When you read, study, and pray the source documents using *lectio divina,* you form much different conclusions from those of mass society and ideological extremists.

Thereby you observe one of Pope Benedict's most frequent counsels regarding Scripture: interpret it within the context of the whole Bible, Tradition, life, and magisterial teachings, rather than according to personal whim, popular opinion, or contemporary ideologies. Pope Benedict has long counseled a critical approach to the Bible, Vatican II, and Catholicism in the true sense of the word, as a search for essence and truth rather than an exercise in negativity, skepticism, and agenda affirmation.

Since John XXIII called the Council, the challenge of following a nuanced, moderate, integrated path has been at odds with mass culture and polarizing factions—just as in New Testament times. This narrow, balanced, middle way was charted by Jesus and has been maintained by the Church. It breeds fullness in the individual and community. As the venerable Latin proverb states, "virtue stands in the middle."

## The New Spiritual Springtime

The "new spiritual springtime" in the Church prophesied by Pope Benedict will occur as a result of our commitment to *lectio divina* in a way that respects both tradition and *aggiornamento* (updating). Fundamentalism rejects nuances and diversity and reduces everything to simple, fundamental principles typically idealogically-driven. It narrows dialogue according to a preconceived agenda. The Bible, *lectio divina*, and life are not conducive to such an approach. Conversely, *lectio divina* of the Bible and magisterial texts such as the above can help us join St. Paul and the communion of saints (cf. Heb 12:1-2) in continuing the race and speeding on with the word.

Mary and Joseph started their marriage on the move, and life with Jesus surely kept them on their toes, so they can help us along the Way—the seminal name for the faith implies movement and a journey (cf. Acts 9:2; 18:26; 19:9, 23; 22:4; 24:14, 22).

Along the Way we need to communicate and work together to continue the dialogue of salvation. One of the greatest impediments to such is the hostility between the genders that has taken institutional and ideological form like never before. In the next chapter, we will apply the dialogical principles of this chapter, using the model of *lectio divina*, to expose the heretical ideologies of our day in the light of the Gospel, and foster a more harmonious lifestyle in obedience to the word and each other.

# – Five –

## The Gender Dimension of *Lectio Divina*
## A Journey with Mary and Joseph

A BOOK on *lectio divina* does not typically include a chapter devoted to gender-related considerations, but after reading this chapter, I hope you'll agree that it should. Such an omission deprives the reader of precious insights into how the counter-cultural witness of Joseph and Mary can inspire and enhance our practice of *lectio divina* and Christian virtues. Joseph and Mary's synthesis of the word of God (spirituality) and life application (morality, praxis, i.e., faith in action) is a model for us.

## Gender and *Lectio Divina*

Throughout this book *lectio divina* has been discussed and grappled with as a multi-dimensional communications, spirituality, and wholeness/wellness model whose applications extend far beyond devotional practice. The communications and wholeness dimensions make *lectio* particularly suited to gender identity, vocation, and collaboration issues.

Like the genders, *lectio* is a paradox and mystery. There are as many ways of practicing *lectio* as there are persons, just as, to quote the French proverb, "as many marriages, that many arrangements." There are also common principles and practices in both *lectio* and gender relationships that we can identify and assimilate in order to optimize our experience and promote peace of mind and soul.

## The Sexual Signs of the Times

Gender relations is a critical area in secular and Church life that has been severely distorted, politicized, and polarized. The catalysts of gender harmony: communication, cooperation, love, and truth have become overshadowed and marginalized by individual rights, expediency, and the tyranny of the strident minority.

Mary and Joseph and *lectio divina* are the finest models for pursuing gender healing and harmony. We will address them frankly, professionally, and pastorally, albeit incompletely. The previous two chapters on discernment (divine and human signs) and dialogue offer guidelines for navigating disagreements and misunderstandings. Unity and reconciliation is possible between and within the genders even amid weakness, wounds, and ambiguity. Like peace, reconciliation must begin with each person, hence the need for the salve and catalyst of *lectio*.

Perhaps the most practical, pastoral, and compulsory reason for addressing the gender dimension of *lectio* is its potential to enhance or disturb our peace and equilibrium. We practice and share *lectio* as sensitive, fragile men and women, and thus any gender-related conflicts or insecurities will impede our relaxation, concentration, and contemplation faculties, and diminish the *lectio* experience.

Gender is the most sensitive and potentially volatile component of dialogue, the most overlooked aspect of spirituality and potential fulfillment, and one of the most controversial and misunderstood aspects of the Bible and Catholicism.

## Reconciliation Within and Between the Genders

There is no better context for reconciliation than Scripture, *lectio divina*, and the Sacraments. The intimate, holistic, developmental, dialogical, and versatile nature of *lectio divina* is particularly suited to gender communications and reconciliation. Flexibility and discernment are necessary for engaging problems at the proper level.

For example, a struggling couple finds counseling and frank discussions to be fruitless. As part of a divine therapy initiative, both commit themselves to consistent practice of *lectio divina* over a significant period of time. Quick results are not the norm in spirituality or sexuality.

The couple can choose or decline to focus on gender-related passages, including those involving Mary and Joseph. Significant benefits of this endeavor include:

1) The couple give themselves time to ride out the wave of dissatisfaction and contentiousness in their relationship. They persevere and open themselves to God and the Church's help and the normal balancing course of events. They ride out the valleys proactively and hopefully, rather than passively and fatalistically. In the meantime, they direct their energies constructively, and avoid the perils of idleness and abstinence identified by St. Paul in 1 Cor 7:5.

In athletic terms, they put themselves in a position to succeed. If counseling and dialogue aren't working, they try a credible alternative. They use the balm of time to allow their relationship to ride out the tumultuous period and enter a more stable stage. If external events are at the root of their conflict, time allows circumstances to pass, and hopefully improve. Of course, there are no guarantees, except of God's love and providence.

2) In a peaceful context, the couple learns about themselves and perhaps their partner through the mirror of Scripture. Self-knowledge and understanding of one's partner diminishes the frequency and potency of projection, whereby our unconscious blind spots are imposed on others and interpreted as a reflection of them rather than us. Of course, human interactions are not cut-and-dried, and in many cases there are multiple factors to consider. Such unpacking requires a competent therapist, whether human or divine. A conjugal commitment to *lectio divina*, whether shared or individual, engages the divine therapist in a humble manner, allowing God to work in His own time and way.

3) Interaction with the word enables the participants to submit themselves to God's judgment rather than their own or their partner's. When our blind spots and shortcomings are exposed

through contact with the Scriptures, we are less likely to seek out and focus on others'.

At the very least, sustained practice of *lectio divina* will soften our hearts, impart perspective, and help us view our situation more clearly and calmly. We can address our problems from a position of strength rather than compulsion and raw emotion.

By practicing *lectio divina* on the texts involving Mary and Joseph, not only in the Bible, but in magisterial documents, through an osmotic process we will gradually begin assimilating and emulating their dispositions, virtues, and service orientation. What finer goal of spiritual and human development than to become more like Mary and Joseph in word and deed? How pleasing this would be to their son and Father!

Contemplating and modeling ourselves after Mary and Joseph effectively bypasses the circular pattern of emotional turmoil, envy, resentment, and pride. The input we feed to our mind, emotions, body, and spirit directly influences the output, our disposition and behavior. If we take in the Holy Family, we won't think, feel, or act like the dysfunctional sitcom, sports, and celebrity personalities held up in the mass media as gender models.

Joseph and Mary were real persons who experienced many of the same trials as us, albeit in different contexts and ways. I will respond differently to friends, peers, and family members of the opposite sex, and the opposite sex in general, if I take the Holy Family as my model and focus on them rather than on fleeting ideologies, social trends, and cultural mores. I will respond better to feminist and macho influences, gender equity initiatives, and personal identity, vocation, and relational issues if I have Mary and Joseph and the word of God as my dynamic frame of reference through an ongoing practice of *lectio divina* and Christian service.

## Breaking the Silence

Frank and balanced discussion of gender issues within both the Church and society has been lacking due in large part to ignorance, fear, apathy, discouragement, and polemical propaganda. A main objective of this chapter is to expose and affirm the wisdom of moderation with respect to both gender issues and the Bible. This can eliminate a lot of conflict, misunderstanding, and grief. We don't have the time or space for a complete treatment, but at least we'll lay a foundation and stimulate a *lectio* response to a confused and disorderly aspect of modern life.

Reconciliation is necessary first within the individual, then within the genders, and finally between them. Individually and communally, we are our own worst enemies. Ultimately there is more contentiousness and sabotage within the ranks than from the perceived adversary.

Popes Paul VI, John Paul II, and Benedict XVI have recognized the critical relevance of biblical teaching on gender issues in their addresses and writings, but the nuances and practical applications of their insights have generally not filtered down to the parish and family level. Generally the secular media has ignored, opposed, repressed, or distorted the message.

## Interpretation Versus Ideology

In its 1993 document, "The Interpretation of the Bible in the Church," the Pontifical Biblical Commission pointed out the dangers of injecting modern ideologies such as feminism into exegesis of the Bible. The potentially divisive nature of this subject was such that several members of the commission requested that their disagreement with the commission's conclusion be disclosed in a footnote.

The imposition of the radical feminist mentality onto the biblical text can lead to a neutering and politicization of the text, thereby diminishing its inspirational and transformational power. Gender-specific biblical passages that contradict feminist doctrines are often dismissed as sexist and either marginalized or subjectively reinterpreted.

The profound spirituality of passages such as the household codes in Eph 5:21-33 is blunted by a superficial and polemical reading more influenced by modern ideology than the Spirit of God.

Both in the academic world and in the public forum many feminine assertions are accorded immunity from critical analysis. Alternative viewpoints are often reflexively branded as misogynist and addressed emotionally and contentiously rather than through reason and dialogue. The same distortions can occur with respect to magisterial teaching and Church discipline. Radicals on both ends of the spectrum can be fundamentalist in their thinking—that is, they oversimplify complex issues out of fear and insecurity. *Lectio divina* provides us with the tools and material (God's word) to develop the maturity and balance necessary for an efficacious faith in today's unstable world (cf. Heb 5:11-14; 1 Cor 3:1-3).

## Ignorance Isn't Bliss

Unfortunately many Church leaders and biblical scholars and teachers are supportive of much of the feminist agenda without being informed on the issues. They are insufficiently acquainted with the professional literature and grassroots reality and are oblivious to feminist repression or lack of respect for dissenting viewpoints in the media, popular culture, academia, and ecclesiastical circles. Their schedules and responsibilities do not allow them to be competent on tangential disciplines in which alternative viewpoints are not readily accessible and cultural pressures to conform are significant. Consequently they are unable to see beyond emotionally charged and sometimes coercive feminist rhetoric and think critically as well as compassionately (recognizing legitimate feminist concerns). Their ignorance and sympathy undercut their goodwill, common sense, and native intelligence. Dialogue on the issues rather than contentiousness and positioning is necessary for mutual enrichment, solidarity, reconciliation, and justice for all concerned.

For example, many women's studies programs, often mislabeled gender studies since the focus is generally one-sided, give insufficient attention to contrasting data and viewpoints. (See the books of Christina Hoff Summers, F. Carolyn Graglia, Warren Farrell, Cornelius F. Murphy, Jr., Paul Nathanson, and Katherine Young for more on this subject.)

How are you going to reconcile with, support, rehabilitate, or build up your counterpart if you don't try to understand and communicate with them on their terms and turf as well as yours? A major aspect of dialogue is finding common ground and shared perspectives and interests. The dialogue of salvation is a communal affair.

Distortion and dismissal of contrary viewpoints and research is contrary to women's as well as men's interests in that it stifles the female propensity towards dialogue, empathy, and conciliation.

## The Catholic Response

The mainstream of Catholic hermeneutics and biblical spirituality lies in the middle: recognizing the historical and cultural context of texts without imposing modern ideologies. Let the text speak for itself, and interpreters for themselves—rather than for the whole Church or even a sub-group (in the case of feminism, women).

The women's movement, which has accomplished so much, regresses into interest group status when it allows radical ideologues that promote unbridled self-interest, suspicion, adversarial and punitive attitudes, and exaggerated notions of independence rather than mutuality and rehabilitation. As is so often the case in revolutions and cultural upheavals, the oppressed become the oppressors.

On a personal level, this can lead to demonizing or calumnizing ("bad-mouthing") of the opposite gender (often, one's current or former partner). *Lectio divina* helps us detect our blind spots, wounds, and hidden agendas through the mirror of the Scriptures and the sword of the Spirit.

Joseph was unwilling to humiliate Mary even though it appeared from his and the law's perspective that she merited such. Mary accepted the damage to her reputation that likely ensued from her miraculous pregnancy. Both put others' needs and God's will above theirs. Gender reconciliation requires similar dispositions.

Just as we cannot say Jesus is Lord except in the Holy Spirit (cf. 1 Cor 13:3), so we cannot understand and assist those whose interests do not seem aligned with ours except through the grace of God and the support of others, namely the Church and the communion of saints, beginning of course with Mary and Joseph.

By its catalyzation and integration of the whole person, body, mind, emotions, and spirit, under the inspiration of the Holy Spirit, *lectio divina* can help us find the language, disposition, and practical initiatives necessary for moving beyond polemics. This essential aspect of the dialogue of salvation was introduced in 1964 in *Ecclesiam Suam* and particularized to gender issues in 2004 in the Sacred Congregation for the Doctrine of the Faith's *Letter to the Bishops of the Catholic Church on the Collaboration Between Men and Women in the Church and the World.*

## Charity Above All

Charitable and pastoral, as well as intellectual and doctrinal considerations need to be factored in. Historically as well as contemporarily (see Archbishop Sheen's discussion of Simone de Beauvoir in the foreword to Jean Guitton's outstanding work, *Feminine Fulfillment*), many of the more radical protagonists in the women's movement bear the scars of abuse or abandonment.

Conversely, countless women who have been hurt deeply and inexcusably by men (and vice-versa) have spurned retribution and chosen the path of compassion, dialogue, forgiveness, reconciliation, and healing. They reach out to others, both victims and victimizers, and thereby become wounded healers.

Unfortunately, their voices and example tend to be eclipsed by extremists whose wounds remain raw and open and who seek remedy and retribution through legal means, public validation, and one-sided, disproportionate social change, measures which may be well-intentioned but in practice are highly vulnerable to manipulation and exploitation.

As Paul VI pointed out in *Evangelii Nuntiandi* ("On Evangelization in the Modern World"), and in accordance with the preaching of Jesus, conversion must always begin and continue with the self. Otherwise reform measures intended for others eventually degenerate into retaliation and positioning and are side-tracked by the underlying self-serving agenda.

Overzealous or misdirected reformers and ideologues can be healed and evangelized according to their needs only after we have first healed and evangelized ourselves. You can't give what you don't have. They deserve respect, consideration, an ear and open heart, and compassion free of patronization and condescension—in short, the dialogical disposition cultivated in *lectio*, articulated by Paul VI, and exemplified by the modern pontiffs. All of us are learning and have our blind spots, so we can't afford to tune anyone out or box anyone in through labels and prejudice.

No matter where we are on these issues, we bear some scars, prejudices, and agenda. We need to look inside ourselves and recognize our own bias, hurt, and hostility in order to avoid projecting it onto others. We will not experience or convey the peace that is a fruit of the Spirit unless we treat those we oppose or disagree with in a dignified and respectful manner. The prayer of St. Francis reminds us to take their side first. In so doing, we foster communication, cooperation, and reconciliation.

## Prudent Expectations and Goodwill

In his spiritual classic, *Introduction to the Devout Life*, St. Francis de Sales counsels us not to occupy ourselves in judging or meddling mentally, emotionally, or socially in the affairs of others. Regardless of where we stand on the aforementioned issues, we need to separate the issue from the person and make allowances for their humanity, that is, extend the benefit of the doubt.

Whenever I dialogue with or attend a presentation by someone whose perspective I disagree with, I try to suspend my bias and agenda. I look for the good rather than the bad, what builds up and forms rather than deforms. If they say something I believe to be incorrect, I make a mental note of it, then let it go. We don't have to agree with everything someone believes or says in order to get along with and learn from them. We can separate the issues from the person and engage in peaceful dialogue and reflection.

## Critical Listening

If I listen critically and compassionately enough to probe the essence of what people are saying, while factoring in their background (a contextual understanding), I will invariably extract something positive, and most likely they will as well. I learn so much about myself whenever I take people on their own terms and appreciate what they have to offer. If even the intimate bond of marriage is not meant to evolve into fusion, much less should I expect precise synchronization with those I relate to on a less familiar basis, particularly initially and when our backgrounds and experiences are disparate.

In contrast to the adversarial approach of contemporary gender polemics is the Bible and particularly the New Testament, where emphasis is placed on advocacy and the Advocate (i.e., Jesus and the Holy Spirit; cf. Jn 14—16) rather than accusation and demonizing—which the scribes and Pharisees did to Jesus, accusing Him of being possessed (cf. Mk 3:22; Jn 8:48-49). The Hebrew word *satan* means accuser or adversary and was used in a legal context as a term for a prosecuting attorney. The Greek word *diabolos* translated as devil means slanderer or accuser. In the discernment process or when we examine our conscience, we might consider whether these definitions are actualized in our behavior.

Unlike some fundamentalist Protestant preachers who have a tidy dogmatic interpretation for a whole slew of texts, the Church is selective in defining the literal meaning of a particular passage of Scripture. It has done so conclusively less than thirty times in its history. The interpretive freedom provided by the Church must be used responsibly, without misleading, offending, or scandalizing others.

With respect to the interpretation and application of gender-related texts, truth and love must be paramount. We should use the approved (see the PBC statement referenced on page 101 for guidance) exegetical tools and resources at our disposal, but without alienating the head from the heart. Quoting St. Ambrose, *Dei Verbum* teaches that prayer must accompany the reading of Scripture, so that God and man may talk together. Such prayer engages the Spirit, Who infuses us with the graces to move beyond ideology and polemics and to emulate Mary and Joseph in being receptive to God's agenda and the needs of others, while subordinating ours.

If we are reading the text from a particular vantage point, such as liberation theology, feminism, or even philosophical perspectives such as phenomenology or Christian personalism (cf. John Paul's Theology of the Body), we need to recognize the eisegetical dimension and avoid imposing conclusions on others. The more we know ourselves, to which *lectio* is an aid, the less likely we will project our immaturities and insecurities upon others. For more on how the aforementioned influence our gender interactions, see John Sanford's *The Invisible Partners: How the Male and Female in Each of Us Affects Our Relationships.* This applies to groups as well as individuals.

## Pastoral Considerations

In accordance with the teaching of St. Paul in the Letters to the Romans and Corinthians, the conscience of each person must be respected. Each person must discern in dialogue with the Spirit and the Church how gender-related teachings apply to their life, and what accommodations fit particular biblical texts. We have to ask probing questions such as the following, and be willing to wrestle with them and accept the consequences:

- Is the patriarchal context, or historical conditioning, of the text so prominent that a literal application to a different cultural and historical milieu is inappropriate?
- If so, what accommodated meaning or application preserves the text's timeless, essential values and relevance?

Many gender-related passages require us to seek a happy medium between rigid literalness and convenient accommodation. The Church takes a middle, pastoral path. It respects various sensitivities and perspectives while pursuing "that truth which God wanted put into sacred writings for the sake of salvation," *Dei Verbum's* (section 11) classic definition of biblical inerrancy.

Bring whatever "word" (insights or applications) you received from this chapter to prayer and to the Church in dialogue. In *lectio divina* and the Church's teachings on gender and on biblical interpretation (exegesis) and accommodation (personal, contemporary application), you have the tools for developing your own reflections and applications. Additional guidance is available in *The St. Joseph Guide to the Bible.*

*Lectio's* uniting of the head and the heart compels us to read and listen critically in the sense of looking for the essential truths of the matter, as Paul VI taught in *Ecclesiam Suam.* We seek areas of agreement and build upon them, while avoiding contentiousness (cf. 1 Cor 11:16). We are called to dialogue in a spirit of love and truth with God, neighbor, and the Church. Love covers a multitude of sins (cf. 1 Pt 4:8). Truth exposes the shortcomings of the modern pathologies of fundamentalism, relativism, and individualism, and most immediately, our own.

## Conclusion

What struck me most in working on this chapter is how gender sensitivities must be incorporated into the larger picture of human nature, morality, and spirituality. As St. Paul said, in Christ there are no divisions, including gender (cf. Gal 3:28). How interesting and paradoxical it is that the more you come to an awareness of gender identity, vocation, and relationship issues, the more intimately you get in touch with your and others' humanity and God's mercy and wisdom.

In the concluding chapters, we will explore how Mary and Joseph can help us assimilate and exemplify in word and deed the spirit of obedience and consecration (giving of ourselves) implicit in *lectio divina* and central to gender, vocational, and relational fulfillment. The words and deeds of biblical characters and teachers, and their disciples, the saints, are more eloquent and efficacious than lengthy sociological or philosophical treatises.

# – Six –

## Receiving the Word with Mary

"THE Virgin Mary has always been proposed to the faithful by the Church as an example to be imitated, not precisely in the type of life she led, and much less for the socio-cultural background in which she lived and which today scarcely exists anywhere. She is held up as an example to the faithful rather for the way in which, in her own particular life, she fully and responsibly accepted the will of God (cf. Lk. 1:38), because she heard the word of God and acted on it, and because charity and a spirit of service were the driving force of her actions. She is worthy of imitation because she was the first and the most perfect of Christ's disciples. All of this has a permanent and universal exemplary value" (*Marialis Cultus* "On the Right Ordering and Development of Devotion to the Blessed Virgin Mary," October 2, 1974, 35).

## Marian Mission

We will discuss the Gospel portrait of Mary with respect to how she practices the various components of *lectio divina* while highlighting her receptivity. Mary bridges the Old and New Testament. The Magnificat (cf. Lk 1:46-55) recalls Hannah's prayer in 1 Sam 2:1-10, and she cooperates with the Spirit in giving Jesus life and receiving life from Him. We will reflect on both the feminine and human dimensions of her availability and responsiveness to the divine will and providence.

## A Modern Marian Creed

On July 30, 1968, exactly five days after the publication of *Humanae Vitae*, Pope Paul VI issued a modern creed. Sadly, it remains largely ignored. The Marian section presented below constitutes a solid theological foundation for our reflections, and a source for *lectio divina.* The final sentence draws attention to Mary's maternal support of our *lectio divina* efforts.

"We believe that Mary is the Mother, who remained ever a Virgin, of the Incarnate Word, our God and Savior Jesus Christ, and that by reason of this singular election, she was, in consideration of the merits of her Son, redeemed in a more eminent manner, preserved from all stain of original sin and filled with the gift of grace more than all other creatures.

"Joined by a close and indissoluble bond to the Mysteries of the Incarnation and Redemption, the Blessed Virgin, the Immaculate, was at the end of her earthly life raised body and soul to heavenly glory and likened to her risen Son in anticipation of the future lot of all the just; and we believe that the Blessed Mother of God, the New Eve, Mother of the Church, continues in heaven her maternal role with regard to Christ's members, cooperating with the birth and growth of divine life in the souls of the redeemed" (Profession of Faith, 'Credo' of the People of God, July 30, 1968).

## Recognizing Gender Distinctions

The Hebrew term *ezer kenegdo* translated as "helper corresponding to him" in the Adam and Eve narrative implies a mirror-like reflection that stands in a complementary and empowering tension with its opposite. The genders share a common humanity and unique individuality as persons, but they are distinct nonetheless.

Drawing upon both Jungian psychology (the concepts of the anima and animus, i.e., the repressed and undeveloped masculine and feminine dimensions in the woman and man respectively) and common sense and experience, we recognize the presence and potential of dimensions of the opposite sex in each of us, and seek to nurture, develop, and respect those in others as well. In this way, we will work towards achieving both personal integration (i.e., potential fulfillment, wellness, in

Jungian terms, individuation) and relationship harmony in accordance with God's will.

By celebrating gender equality, differences, complementarities, interdependence, vocations, and potentialities while acknowledging their limitations and vulnerabilities, we adopt the mindset of the Bible, which does not equate equality with equivalence. With these preliminaries in mind, we are ready to address the question of how Mary practiced *lectio divina* in a distinctly feminine as well as prototypically human way.

## Meditating on Mary with a Master

Both from a practical and conceptual standpoint, it seems best to adopt the approach taken by Pope Paul VI in *Marialis Cultus* of focusing on Mary in the liturgy and in Scripture, while taking into account ecumenical and anthropological considerations. Thus we join Mary in attentiveness to the Word of God received in Scripture and the Eucharist.

A complete picture of modern papal teaching on Mary would obviously extend beyond Paul VI. However, *Marialis Cultus* is so focused, balanced, and accessible that it seemed like a good introduction and sampling. Further, I have written a book on Paul VI and have a Paul VI library at my disposal, so I feel comfortable synthesizing his thought.

On November 21, 1964, Pope Paul gave Mary the title of Mother of the Church after he promulgated the "Dogmatic Constitution on the Church" *Lumen Gentium*, which featured Mary in its closing chapter. He is a modern prophet, spiritual master, and outstanding teacher of Mariology. He wrote several encyclicals on her as well.

## Marian Meditations

A complete exegesis and exposition of Mary's role in the Bible is beyond the scope of this chapter. Accordingly, let us focus on "words" or themes to identify with her and discover her *lectio* lessons. I will provide brief reflections and questions designed to facilitate *lectio divina* on Mary and in particular her modeling of *lectio divina*. We will conclude with a synthesis of biblical passages on Mary from Pope Paul VI that is conducive to both *lectio divina* and catechetics.

Add any "words" or themes I have not included, or amend or expand upon my reflections and questions. Consider making this a Marian journal in which you contemplate her service of the Word and the applications to your life.

## Receptivity

"*Fiat*, let it be done to me according to your word."

Mary heard the word and carried it out. Maternity, receptivity to life at its conception and inception, and the accompanying nurturing and care-giving dispositions, are seminal examples of the feminine dimension of this characteristic.

- *Do I "bloom where I am planted" and accept the constraints of life without becoming passive or fatalistic, making the best of my situation and talents?*

- *Do I experience life appreciatively, looking for the silver lining and entrusting myself to God, even when my emotions and instincts dictate otherwise?*

- *Do I receive others as they are, God as He is, the Church as it is, and myself as I am, humbly, hopefully, and lovingly, or do I insist on them and myself conforming to my rules, agenda, and desires, even to the point of aggression and other controlling or manipulative behaviors? What wounds, faults, or circumstances underlie my indiscretions, insecurities, or immaturities?*

- *Do I receive the Bible as it is, wrestling with those texts that do not sit well with me, or do I avoid or rationalize the tough parts?*

- *Am I willing to enter fully into the experience of suffering, unpleasant as it may be, rather than stay at the surface or run away (i.e., engage in evasive or anesthetizing activities or rationalizations), and thereby experience the joy and peace beyond understanding (cf. Gal 4:7) that lies at the other end?*

- *Am I receptive to suffering and the lessons and meaning it entails while doing all I can to mitigate it with appropriate remedies?*

**Patient Contemplation**

"Mary kept all these things and pondered them in her heart" (cf. Lk 2:19).

Mary intuitively responded rather than impulsively reacted to God's word as communicated by the Angel and in the person of Jesus. She stored and nurtured rather than dismissed the human and divine signs. In this way, she stored up riches (cf. Sir 3:4), just as Jesus did in His obedience to her.

Mary's patience contrasts with the harsh impulsiveness of Job's wife, who is unable to control her disappointment and anger, thereby bringing down her husband (cf. Job 2:7-8). Even a holy couple such as Anna and Tobit bickered under pressure (cf. Tob 2:11—3:1). Abraham and Sarah had their rough spots. Mary gave God's word time to grow and accomplish its purpose. She did not yield to the conditionings of her environment but instead chose to accept the demands and constraints of God's word.

- *Do I allow the word the time it requires? Do I stay with the word, or with others, allowing them the time to blossom, recognizing that God's and others' timelines may not be mine? Do I allow others the time they need even when it is inconvenient or trying, including when I don't receive acknowledgment or appreciation?*

- *Do I have an ongoing dialogical, reflective relationship with God, others, myself, and life, thereby enabling the Spirit to guide me in recognizing the signs of the times and my life? Do I open myself to the divine and human*

*signs that come to me in both* lectio *and life? Do I wrestle with them even when they push me out of my comfort zone?*

- *Do I seek the intercession and consolation of Mary and
Joseph, and the inspirational value of their example, particularly when I join them in following God's will into
uncertainty and insecurity?*

- *What are the interior (within me) and external (circumstantial, worldly) obstacles to my discernment and
responsiveness to divine and human signs?*

**Attentiveness**

Mary reflexively and thoughtfully responded to the particulars of the situation and the needs of others through compassionate awareness: "They have no wine"—*lectio divina* in
action.

Attentiveness is so obviously a feminine trait that it is frequently overlooked. My speaking experience testifies to this.
My practical needs are typically addressed proactively by
women: the water at the podium, the temperature of the room,
the distribution of the handouts, the inquiry as to whether I
have any unmet needs. If my hair is mussed, my collar rum-
pled, or my shirt untucked, I can count on a woman to bring it
gently to my attention. I often get the impression that they
enjoy being of assistance. I have known men to anticipate and
address these situations, but the way the genders go about this
typically differs.

- *Do I pay attention to the little things in the Bible that
make a difference, e.g., repeated words, interwoven
themes, correspondences / agreements / complementarities between different texts in the Bible, compelling grammatical expressions or phrasing, explicit links with my life
experience and challenges, or do I stay at the surface?*

- *Do I go through my day being attentive to others and to
situations, opening myself to the Spirit's promptings and*

*taking the risks that involvement in other people's lives entails?*

## Detachment

Mary gave of herself in order to be an obedient and pliable "earthen vessel" (cf. 2 Cor 4:7) of God's will and providence.

Women (and men) are capable of great sacrifices for a cause. One of the most regrettable offenses of radical feminism is its emphasis on narrow self-fulfillment at the expense of outreach to others and commitment to the common good. Giving oneself in *lectio* and not allowing ourselves to be possessed by competing distractions (e.g., possessions, banal pastimes, hyperactivity, superficial gratifications) enables us to be fully disposed to God and His word.

Mary is not possessive of Jesus. Like any mother she had to learn to let go of her son. We observe this tension at Cana, where as a good Jewish mother she wants her son to make a situation right when it is within His power. We encountered this inclination initially at the finding of the adolescent Jesus in the temple, where Mary reproves Him while also listening to Him and expanding her horizons with respect to His identity and mission. She knows how to dialogue, and invites us to join her.

- *Am I possessive of my spirituality or loved ones? Do I react harshly when I am interrupted or thrown off my schedule or agenda? Do I share myself and those dear to me even at the risk of rejection, inconvenience, or disappointment?*

- *Do I engage in the sacrifices that the word entails, such as giving up an enjoyable pursuit in order to be with God or others in service?*

- *Do I share my resources, e.g., lending spiritual books or other goods to those who need but perhaps cannot afford them, fully recognizing that they will likely not be returned intact or in a timely manner, if at all?*

- *Am I possessive of my faith or do I give it away, spending the time necessary to engage in interfaith, ecumenical, catechetical, and reconciliatory dialogue and other cooperative endeavors?*

**Transparency**

At Cana Mary goes directly to Jesus and the servants, becoming involved and vulnerable to rejection or rebuke in a situation that does not specifically concern her, at least on the surface. She refuses to hide behind masks, games, conventions, or formalities. She grasps the essential elements of a person or situation, and is willing to dialogue honestly even at the risk of rebuttal or misunderstanding (e.g., the exchanges at Cana and on finding Jesus in the temple). Mary reminds us of Thomas Merton's insight that it is more important to be sincere than to be right.

- *When I apply and live what I receive in* lectio divina, *do I put myself out there and expose myself to criticism or misunderstandings? Am I willing to be transparent with God and others, including in confession, or do I hide behind masks and play games out of fear of exposing the real me?*

**Humble Perseverance**

One of the biblical passages in which the benefits of redaction criticism are most apparent is when Mary and Jesus' "brothers"are calling for Jesus. In Mark's Gospel, they think He is out of His mind, and Jesus proclaims that His mother and brothers are those who obey God's word (cf. Mk 3:21, 31-35). The emphasis is on discipleship rather than on Mary's fidelity, though the latter is not excluded, of course.

In Luke's Gospel, Jesus pays tribute to His mother in response to a woman in the crowd who praises Mary's physical maternity. Jesus instead praises Mary's receptivity to God's word (cf. Lk 11:27-28). Clearly Luke either has a more favorable view of Mary, or simply accords her more attention. Like us and her husband, Mary doesn't always get the attention and credit she merits.

One challenging aspect of the *lectio divina* experience is accepting the anonymity and frustration that accompanies it. We try hard, and sometimes the fruits aren't apparent, at least to us. Mary and Joseph struggled in the dark at times, like we do. They can be effective intercessors when we encounter such difficulties.

Many persons of both sexes labor in the dark or in the background. Members of both sexes operate in the shadows and margins due to economic or social discrimination. Mary manifests a humble, gentle response worthy of emulation by both sexes. Fidelity to God's word will not always bring us a pat on the back in this life. More often than not, as with Mary, it brings us a pierced or broken heart.

- *Do I approach* lectio *like I should the Mass, being less concerned with what I get out of it than with what I put into it? Am I willing to endure the dryness, ambiguity, and confusion that accompany God's word?*

- *Am I willing to spurn human recognition in favor of divine?*

## Mutuality and Respect

Mary parents with Joseph in a fluid, cooperative manner. She addresses Jesus respectfully but quizzically when they find Him in the temple, and speaks in solidarity with Joseph, saying "Your father and I" (cf. Lk 2:41-51).

- *Am I civil, inclusive, and respectful in my interactions with those who perplex or challenge me? Do I operate autonomously, or in cooperation and dialogue with others?*

- *Do I let the Scriptures inform my dispositions and language towards others, or am I passively conditioned by the world?*

**Compassionate Suffering**

Mary is with Jesus until the end, sharing in His suffering in fulfillment of the prophecy of Simeon ("a sword will pierce your heart"; cf. Lk 2:34-35). Apparently Joseph has died, and she lives the vulnerability of a widow. Now she loses her only son.

Mary knows deprivation and loss. She retains her dignity amid it. She listens to the word even when in human terms it disappoints her. She realizes that we have not a lasting city here, but looks for one that is to come (cf. Heb 13:14). Our *lectio divina* should likewise keep our minds on what is above (cf. Col 3:2). The Church uses this passage in the Easter morning liturgy to remind us of the perspective we should maintain.

- *Am I willing to practice* lectio divina *when I am tired, bored, or discouraged, and respond to God's word obediently in life even when it is inconvenient and costs me something? Do I accept the affliction that accompanies the word (cf. 1 Thes 1:6), or do I rebel to the point of giving up the dialogue and attentiveness?*

**Solidarity with the Community**

Mary gathers in the Upper Room with the Apostles, united in prayer and fellowship (cf. Acts 1:13-14). She does not seek special attention or privilege, but rather immerses herself into the community. Her actions remind us that the primary forum for *lectio divina* is the Mass, and the most practical resource, the lectionary. When we hear the word proclaimed and share it with others, and receive nourishment from fellowship and the Eucharist, we experience God's word on multiple levels. Mary flows with the word, and does not separate it from the community.

The concept of *sola scriptura* (Scripture alone) would be foreign to Mary. Mary's responsiveness to God's word is not a matter of legalistic, literalistic, or eclectic adhesion, but of fluid, dialogical, liberating obedience. This liberation comes at a cost, but Mary is willing to pay it, not out of morbidity or a compulsive sense of duty, but out of love.

- *Am I a* lectio *Lone Ranger or do I seek out Bible-sharing groups or classes so that I may learn from and with others and give of myself as well? Do I experience the Bible as a community document, or am I possessive of it, interpreting and applying it narrowly according to my agenda?*

## Devotional Diversity

The late Cistercian writer and proponent of Centering Prayer, Fr. Basil Pennington, in his book *Mary Today* included numerous testimonies to her from the faithful. The diversity of approaches to Mary was very interesting, and one noted certain patterns along gender lines as well.

One of the most compelling testimonies for me was from a priest who had an aversion to certain forms of Marian devotion more prevalent before Vatican II and traditionally associated with women. His discovery of Paul VI's Apostolic Exhortation *Marialis Cultus* opened up a whole new world to him, a relationship to Mary rooted in liturgy, community, and Scripture, while also being nourished by devotions.

Everyone relates to Mary in a different way, as they do their own mother. I feel comfortable with Joseph, but am put off by saccharine Marian hyperbole that distances me from her by making her seem superhuman and inaccessible. I relate to her as *theotokos* (God-bearer, mother of God), faithful spouse of Joseph, mother of sorrows and of the Church (the pre-eminent disciple), and my sister (cf. Acts 1:14) and maternal intercessor in Christ.

I have an aversion to syrupy approaches to Mary that seem to obscure her humanity and Jesus' centrality. I don't like when Mary is described in overly sentimental, exalted language that makes her seem remote and plastic. Sometimes such overly-reverential treatment spills over into Christology, inadvertently eclipsing Jesus' humanity as well. That is why I identified with the reaction of the aforementioned priest. Of course, I make no judgment on the Mariology or devotional life of others, and instead try to work out my relationship with her in fellowship with the Spirit.

Conversely, I relate well to Joseph because the biblical texts that refer to him so explicitly emphasize his masculine qualities and virtues, and as discussed in the final chapter, the popes and saints who have written on St. Joseph have tended not to obscure his humanity, thereby making him very approachable. He comes across as a real man who stands in stark contrast to the false images of fatherhood and masculinity which are so prevalent today.

One of the benefits of *lectio divina* is that it can help us humanize Mary and Jesus, and therefore make them real to us. Such humanization actually requires more of us, because it cuts off the escape hatches of emotionalism, sentimentality, and angelism (making them so remote and other-worldly that their relevance to us is primarily indirect and impersonal). It is much more challenging and efficacious to dialogue with a person than a concept.

In emulation of its mother who accepted so much in her life in a humble, tolerant, inclusive, and persevering manner, the Church permits a broad range of Mariology and devotions. At the cross Mary received the beloved disciple from her son and thereby allowed her maternity to expand to the whole Church, eventually transcending time and space. *Marialis Cultus* and other documents by Paul VI (he wrote several encyclicals on Mary) and John Paul II provide clear guidelines for ensuring the theological and pastoral efficacy of Marian devotions.

The best way to sum up our survey of Mary and *lectio divina* is with Pope Paul's concise synthesis of biblical testimony to Mary. I have broken it out line by line with the intention of encouraging you to do *lectio divina* on the texts that speak to you. Each of the bulleted phrases can serve as "words" in your *lectio.*

As mentioned previously, papal writings that draw extensively from Scripture are excellent sources for *lectio divina*, as long as we don't become so enamored of papal insight that we lose sight of their foundation, the Scriptures. Papal writings are invaluable for the light they shed on the literal, hinted, applied, and in some cases, mystical levels of meaning in Scripture. (See the discussion of the *pardes* model in chapters one and seven.) This constitutes an excellent exegetical foundation. Thus when we personalize Scripture, we do so on solid interpretive ground.

## *Lectio Divina* on Mary with Paul VI

"The Blessed Virgin's exemplary holiness encourages the faithful to 'raise their eyes to Mary who shines forth before the whole community of the elect as a model of the virtues.' It is a question of solid, evangelical virtues:

- faith and the docile acceptance of the Word of God (cf. Lk 1:26-38, 45; 11:27-28; Jn 2:5);

- generous obedience (cf. Lk 1:38);

- genuine humility (cf. Lk 1:39-56);

- profound wisdom (cf. Lk 1:29, 34; 2:19, 33, 51);

- worship of God manifested in alacrity in the fulfillment of religious duties (cf. Lk 2:21-41) and in gratitude for gifts received (cf. Lk 1:46-49) and in her offering in the Temple (cf. Lk 2:22-24) and in her prayer in the midst of the apostolic community (cf. Acts 1:12-14);

- her fortitude in exile (cf. Mt 2:13-23) and (her fortitude) in suffering (cf. Lk 2:34-35, 49; Jn 19:25);

- her poverty, reflecting dignity and trust in God (cf. Lk 1:48; 2:24);

- her attentive care for her son, from His humble birth to the ignominy of the cross (cf. Lk 2:1-7; Jn 19:25-27);

- her delicate forethought (cf. Jn 2:1-11);

- her virginal purity (cf. Mt 1:18-25; Lk 1:26-38);
- her strong and chaste married love (*Marialis Cultus*, 57).

These virtues of the Mother will also adorn her children who steadfastly study her example in order to reflect it in their own lives. And this progress in virtue will appear as the consequence and the already mature fruit of that pastoral zeal which springs from devotion to the Blessed Virgin."

- *Am I willing to reflect on Mary's example and follow in her contemplative and receptive footsteps, reflecting on these things in my heart and putting them into practice amid darkness and difficulties?*

- *Am I willing to learn* lectio *from the maternal master by nurturing the word and others and accepting the consequences—uncontrollable, unexpected, and disconcerting as they may be?*

- *Am I willing to engage Mary and Joseph in prayer and imaginative dialogue, seeking their intercession, guidance, support, and consolation? Am I willing to relate to them as my spiritual parents? If not, what is keeping me from a closer relationship with Jesus' parents? What can I do to bridge the gap and overcome the obstacles?*

Why not start or continue your *lectio* journey with the above quotations, giving each of them ample consideration and letting them percolate in your heart? Grow closer to Mary by growing closer to the word.

In the next and final chapter, we'll engage her beloved husband.

# – Seven –

## Responding to the Word with Joseph

ST. Joseph and St. Peter were having an argument in heaven about the qualifications necessary for admission into the kingdom. Joseph favored mercy, and Peter went by the Book. Their discussion reached an impasse, at which point the Rock waved his keys at the Guardian and asked him to leave. The imperturbable Saint calmly consented, while adding that of course he would take his son and wife with him. Apparently knocking the Rock and setting him straight runs in the family.

Our *lectio* model in this final chapter is the guardian not only of the Redeemer but of the universal church (in theological terms, patron). The following observations are culled from Pope John Paul II's 1989 Apostolic Exhortation *Redemptoris Custos* ("Guardian of the Redeemer"):

"In bestowing upon St. Joseph the title of universal patron during a difficult time in Church history, Pope Pius XII observed that 'the Church, after the Blessed Virgin, his spouse, has always held him in great honor and showered him with praise, having recourse to him amid tribulations.' In his encyclical *Quamquam Pluies*, Pope Leo XIII exhorted the Church to seek St. Joseph's protection, referring to him as 'the provident guardian of the divine Family.' "

Pope John XXIII had a great devotion to St. Joseph and even invoked papal privilege to pull a few strings for him. He directed that St. Joseph's name be inserted in the Roman Canon of the Mass after the name of Mary but before the apostles, popes, and martyrs. That's good company!

In an audience given on the feast of St. Joseph, March 19, 1969, Pope Paul VI invoked St. Joseph's patronage:

"The Church also calls upon Joseph as her protector because of a profound and ever-present desire to reinvigorate her ancient life with true evangelical virtues, such as shine forth in St. Joseph." In this chapter we'll reflect on these virtues in relation to our practice of *lectio divina*. Suffice it to say that in the communion of saints, Joseph may not be in a class by himself, but it doesn't take long to call roll.

## A Teresian Tribute

As articulate and inspiring as the popes are with respect to this silent saint, they still can't match Teresa of Jesus. (It seems only fitting that the spouse of the Virgin would be honored most eloquently by the saintly Spanish virgin of the Counter-Reformation. As discussed below, both sexes find their greatest praise and challenge from the opposite sex).

Eminently charismatic and persuasive, St. Teresa of Avila encouraged devotion to St. Joseph in the Carmelite reforms. The first female doctor of the Church, and the source of one of the most humorous and poignant laments in Church history: "If this is how You (God) treat Your friends, then it is no wonder You have so few of them," speaks convincingly of St. Joseph in her autobiography:

"I took for my advocate and lord the glorious Saint Joseph and commended myself earnestly to him; and I found that my father and lord delivered me both from this trouble [a temporary paralysis] and also from other and greater troubles concerning my honor and the loss of my soul, and that he gave me greater blessings than I could ask of him. I do not remember even now that I have ever asked anything of him which he has failed to grant. I am astonished at the great favors which God has bestowed on me through this blessed saint, and at the perils from which He has freed me, both in body and in soul.

"To other saints the Lord seems to have given grace to succor us in some of our necessities but of this glorious saint my experience is that he succors us in them all and that the Lord wishes to teach us that as He was Himself subject to him on earth (for, being His guardian and being called His father, he could command Him) just so in Heaven He still does all that he asks. This has also been the experience of other persons whom I have advised to commend themselves to him; and even today there are many who have great devotion to him through having newly experienced this truth.

"I wish I could persuade everyone to be devoted to this glorious saint, for I have great experience of the blessings which he can obtain from God. I have never known anyone to be truly devoted to him and render him particular services who did not notably advance in virtue, for he gives very real help to souls who commend themselves to him. For some years now, I think, I have made some request of him every year on his festival and I have always had it granted. If my petition is in any way ill directed, he directs it aright for my greater good."

How ironic that this chapter which invokes the silent saint in a supporting role would turn out to be the longest in the book—and the final word on the subject. The Gospel narratives begin with Joseph, so it seems fitting to end there too. St. Joseph reminds us that if our actions are right, we won't need to blow our own horn. Others will see and say what lies hidden and what will be revealed at the last judgment (cf. Mt 25:31-46). The merciful just in this parable remind us of the just man, Joseph, the first disciple in Matthew's Gospel.

## The Road of Redemption Runs Through Joseph

For Matthew, the new phase of salvation history inaugurated by Jesus is announced to and essentially runs through Joseph, in circumstances only cryptically anticipated in the Old Testament. The Son of God entered human history in the most inconceivable fashion, under the guise of an illegitimate pregnancy. The curiosity, confusion, and consternation that this evokes can be an entrée into the deeper truths revealed in the mysterious birth of Jesus.

*Lectio divina* is an ideal process for engaging in a dialogue with God about the perplexing events in our life. Just as spouses foster intimacy through sharing themselves and talking through and working out their difficulties, so we grow closer to God by dialoging with Him with our whole selves. In section ten of *Salvifici Doloris* ("On the Christian Meaning of Human Suffering"), Pope John Paul II affirmed the efficacy of the "Why?" question in response to suffering: "Man can put this question to God with all the emotion of his heart and with his mind full of dismay and anxiety; and God expects the question and listens to it. . . ."

## Actions Speak Louder Than Words

St. Joseph is the quiet man in the biblical and Catholic tradition. He says not a word in the Bible, and in Catholic theology and spirituality takes a back seat to Mary. However, this subordination is present in neither Matthew nor Mark, both of which exhibit masculine attributes (e.g., stark realism, directness, intensity, immediacy, a greater emphasis on justice and literal truth than pastoral sensitivity and psychological subtlety, a tendency towards reasoning rather than intuition) and do not emphasize the role of women in Jesus' ministry as prominently as Luke and John do.

Joseph exemplifies obedience to and implementation of God's word amid the obstacles and ambiguities of life. His responsive activism offers a wonderful complement to Mary's contemplative receptivity. He offers an example of the action stage in the concrete circumstances of life.

## The Balancing Act in *Lectio*

One of the arts we cultivate in both *lectio divina* and life is that of balancing the contemplative and activist components. Recalling the disciples of Bethany, we want to keep the inclinations of Mary and Martha in a healthy tension within ourselves.

The action component in *lectio divina* reminds us to seek continuity between our devotional and liturgical lives and our apostolic vocation. It is not enough to hear and believe the word; we must carry it out—in St. Paul's terminology, faith working through love (cf. Gal 5:6). As discussed in chapter two, observance of the Sabbath by not only resting but reflecting on the word of God and God's initiative in our life helps us to keep things in perspective and balance and prepare ourselves for the activities of the week. We want to avoid extremes in both directions.

## The Obedience of Faith

St. Joseph offers a multitude of lessons with regards to both life and *lectio divina*. He illustrates the importance of obeying God's word even when it is confounding, upsetting, inconvenient, and even life-threatening.

Not only St. Joseph's example, but the texts about him reveal core aspects of God's word and will. Above all we are reminded that God's ways are not ours (cf. Isa 55:8). He does not act in conformity to our will and agenda. Nor do events unfold as we would like them to, even when we are trying to serve God.

Such obedience requires letting go of our agenda and submitting ourselves to God's mysterious will. St. Joseph reminds us that when we engage in *lectio*, it is not how much we understand Scripture that is of utmost importance, but how disposed we are to accept and implement it. This Joseph does, along with Mary, in unparalleled fashion.

An eloquent exposition of St. Joseph's modeling of the "obedience of faith" (cf. Rom 1:5; 16:26; 2 Cor 10:5-6) can be found in Pope John Paul II's aforementioned Apostolic Exhortation *Redemptoris Custos*, ("Guardian of the Redeemer"), which was published on the feast of the Assumption, August 15. As Pope John Paul points out, Joseph shares in Mary's glory, and is tied to her in the closest possible manner. *Redemptoris Custos'* exposition of Scripture and the merits and role of St. Joseph makes it a suitable source for *lectio divina*, whereby we benefit from the Pope's insights.

Further, as pointed out by John Paul II, Vatican II's *Dei Verbum* ("Dogmatic Constitution on Divine Revelation"), begins by putting forth the fundamental disposition of the Church, "hearing the word of God with reverence,"which is "an absolute readiness to serve faithfully God's salvific will revealed in Jesus. Already at the beginning of human redemption, after Mary, we find the model of obedience made incarnate in St. Joseph, the man known for having faithfully carried out God's commands (*Redemptoris Custos*, 30)."

Thus Mary and Joseph illustrate a seminal actualization of *lectio divina* in their responsiveness to the word received from the Angels and then The Word, Jesus. As we link *lectio divina* to life through practical applications and actions and an ongoing dialogue with God and those around us, we encounter the Word in its human disguise, the Church, the body of Christ, and our neighbor, particularly those who are suffering (cf. Mt 25:31-46).

## Faithfulness in Little Things

As discussed in chapter two, the Little Way of St. Thérèse Lisieux is particularly relevant to *lectio divina*. We adopt a particularist approach to the Bible and ourselves, focusing on a small portion of Scripture or a particular aspect of our disposition, behavior, or lifestyle. In this way we engage the word and ourselves in a concrete, practical, manageable, and accountable manner, and are not overwhelmed. The obedience of faith in reference to *lectio* can manifest itself when we engage the text and our lives as they are in the present moment, rather than as we'd like them to be, and respond humbly and faithfully in little ways.

We know that it is often more difficult to cope with life's ongoing annoyances and daily trials than to endure traumatic events that periodically come our way. The alienation and discouragement experienced in everyday difficulties contrasts with the comfort and support received amid major loss and tragedy.

## True *Lectio* Doesn't Run Smooth

I often fall asleep when I try to practice *lectio*. I'm still waiting for an angelic message in my dreams. The only thing I end up with is drowsiness. Being intense, efficiency-conscious, and production-oriented (with a name like Karl Schultz, what do you expect?), I strive to accept rather than fight it. When I nod off, I recognize that I need more rest and less stress. Common sense and prudence are also part of the *lectio divina* experience, which is intrinsically connected to our life as a whole—body, mind, spirit, functional, and social. Relationships, life, the Bible, and the Church come together as the source of my inspiration, conversation, and consolation.

We don't practice *lectio* in a vacuum. We experience it in the concrete circumstances of our life. There is usually a residual effect from the ebb and flow of our life. For example, when I get frustrated and discouraged due to negative life events and circumstances, I feel disconnected from God and confused or even alienated from divine providence. The Lament Psalms, Job, Moses, and Jeremiah express similar sentiments. This affects my *lectio* experience, positively or negatively, depending on my disposition and response.

Unless I am vigilant and persevering, the unpleasant taste in my mouth can lead to hardness of heart (resistance to God's word and will). Conversely, if I keep at it and face the core issues that confront me, I often am able to reach a deeper level of intimacy with God and a greater degree of self-knowledge. To use Jesus' analogy in Jn 16:21, in the spiritual maturation process, the pain gives way to joy.

If I sense that my resistance and distractions are impeding the *lectio* process, I won't give up completely, but I'll modify the process. I'll shorten the length of the passage or the time allocated to increase my attentiveness. Sometimes I'll reach for another book in hopes that it will be an enjoyable and restorative digression. Either way, I commit myself to coming back to the *lectio* process soon, lest I get out of the habit.

I discipline myself to engage in such diversions only briefly, and then return to the Bible. I try to be patient with myself and accepting of circumstances beyond my control which affect my dialogue with the Lord. I don't force things or pressure myself to the point of exhaustion, discouragement, or resentment, while at the same time exercising reasonable self-discipline. I try to read and pray with the Bible even when I don't feel like it, recognizing that feelings are not to be equated with faith, while avoiding the extreme of forcing myself beyond my tolerance level.

During dry periods, I await consolation, the peace beyond understanding (cf. Phil 4:8) that is a gift of the Holy Spirit and a fruit of *lectio divina.* Cardinal Martini's inclusion of consolation in his "School of the Word" model of *lectio divina* recognizes the importance of experiencing some form of progress or confirmation during our practice. Otherwise, over the long term discouragement might lead us to practice *lectio* less or not at all. Consolation keeps our dialogue from becoming a monologue.

I believe that if I remain receptive and properly disposed morally (i.e., I continue trying to follow Joseph's example of integrity, justice, mercy, and humility), in His own time and way God will console, affirm, and sustain me for the journey. I make no pretense of standing on my own (cf. 1 Cor 10:12).

When things get really bad, I bring out the heavy artillery. Prime texts from the Gospels, Romans 8, 1 Cor 13, Hebrews 11-13, and inspirational psalms and passages from the prophets. The word becomes a sword of the Spirit, fighting off my opponents as my impeccable Advocate.

1 Cor 15:19 becomes my mantra: "If it is for just this life that we have hoped in Christ, we are the most pitiable of all men." A spiritual splash of cold water may not make me feel better, but it does bring me to reality. For a compelling compendium of biblical inspiration on hope, reference Pope Benedict's 2007 encyclical *Spe Salvi* ("Saved by Hope").

Just as no amount of preparation and effort can insulate a marriage from surprises and disappointments, likewise, no amount of sanctity, goodwill, learning, or maturity can keep the Scriptures from being dry at times. Even popes, saints, and apostles have their bad days. St. Joseph did, and he didn't have a dysfunctional personality or family to blame it on!

## Less Can Be More

Another *lectio* lesson we can derive from Joseph's initial encounter with the Angel is that God can pack a lot into a little. Matthew's description of Joseph's dilemma is a masterpiece of concise understatement. Here we have a man in an unprecedented conundrum, and the biblical narrator describes it impassively and without elaboration. No contrived emotionalism or drama, no literary elegance as in the annunciation to Mary. The annunciation to Joseph is rendered in a straightforward, matter-of-fact manner. No abstractions or platitudes, just the salient points.

## Reading the Bible as a Man or Woman

Just as Mary reveals to us the dignity and possibilities of femininity, so Joseph teaches us about masculinity—in terms that starkly contrast with our macho culture. Both sexes profit from learning about the qualities of the opposite gender, and appropriating them in accordance with their own gifts and vocation.

Each of us engage the Bible from the framework of our experience, circumstances, and identity, which includes our sexuality. The more we get in touch with the dynamic role our masculine or feminine identity, tendencies, and potentialities play in our interaction with God's word, the more whole, perceptive, and responsive we can be.

For example, Joseph is described as just and merciful. He teaches me about being a man and a male disciple, and fulfilling my vocation in life. I react to Joseph's plight out of my masculine identity but also as a human being. While he is a model of authentic masculinity, he also exemplifies human virtues that are equally present in femininity, albeit in different forms. We are not only men and women, but whole persons and unique human beings.

One insight that has been helpful for me is acceptance of my intense, action-oriented approach to the text. I am not gifted with the capacity for deep contemplation, at least so far, but because of my background I am able to discover helpful insights into the text and link these to various aspects of my life.

Conversely, I know many people of both sexes, but particularly women, who are able to center themselves peacefully on the text and experience the contemplative dimension bountifully. Historically, this charism is observable in the many female mystics in the Church, with Mary being the first one. I recognize in this the maternal capacity for focused attentiveness and identification with a subject.

If I am a woman, I can also profit from Joseph's exemplification of the nobler masculine attributes. The more I understand what a man is called to be, the more I will look for, encourage, and support those qualities in the boys and men I interact with. No man achieves fulfillment independent of female support and interaction, and vice-versa. Further, using John Paul II's reciprocal ethics (whereby he takes passages addressed to one sex and deduces applications for the other sex), I appropriate aspects of Joseph's disposition and responsiveness that are relevant to me.

An overlooked aspect of our journey with the Bible is the increasing awareness we can cultivate of the influence of our sexuality on the interpretation, assimilation, and implementation process. Both the Bible and Catholicism recognize the distinctiveness of the sexes in every aspect of life.

Modern science, along with experience and tradition, has revealed to us the depth and breadth of these distinctions in the area of communications, which is a constitutive dimension of the *lectio* experience. For a fuller treatment of the subject, see

Cardinal Carlo Martini, S.J.'s *Communicating Christ to the World*, a collection of his pastoral letters on culture and communication.

The subjectivity of these distinctions and the uniqueness of individuals, along with the common element of our humanity, make rigid generalizations imprudent and untenable, though tendencies and patterns can be identified. The holistic nature of *lectio*, and its incorporation of spontaneity, creativity, and individuality complement and undergird the gender dimension of the undertaking.

## The Dynamic Nature of the Word

In *lectio*, as in Catholic and biblical spirituality in general, we do not want to remain at the level of platitude or abstraction. We want to take the word in and live it, thereby enabling God to transform us through it.

*Lectio* can work with a small dose of content and context. St. Joseph received God's word in his dreams; we may be inspired while reading a brief Bible passage or while interacting with someone on a bus or in a waiting room. Divine providence, like the word of God, cannot be confined or chained (cf. 2 Tim 2:9). Just one line of Scripture can spiritually satiate us and lead us into a deeper encounter with ourselves, God, and others. However, our primary communication partner is always God. If we lose sight of this, our exercise can evolve into a psychological, sociological, or humanistic endeavor, thereby depriving us of the spiritual ends for which *lectio* is primarily intended.

## Silence Can Be Golden

Just as God can work through a paucity of words, likewise there is no requirement that we be eloquent, profound, or verbose in our response. Joseph is the prototype of taciturn responsiveness, the Christian antithesis of the violent anti-hero of the "spaghetti westerns" of the 1960s.

Jesus concludes the Sermon on the Mount with a reminder that it is not boisterous enthusiasm, prophetic insight, or spiritual sophistication, but practical obedience, that matters most (cf. Mt 7:15-29). The repentant second son, not the superficially acquiescent first son, did the father's will (cf. Mt 21:28-32).

Mary recites the Magnificat, while Joseph responds in silence and in deed; both accomplish the will of the Father. There are many paths to God. Everyone has their own gifts and calling. Further, our experience of *lectio* can evolve with time, growth, and circumstances. God's word and providence are dynamic rather than static.

## Mercy Triumphs Over Judgment (cf. Jas 2:13)

In my *lectio* on this profound passage (cf. Mt 1:18-25), I only get as far as the first two verses and am stopped in my tracks:

"The birth of Jesus Christ occurred in this way. When his mother Mary was engaged to Joseph, but before they came to live together, she was found to be with child through the Holy Spirit. Her husband Joseph was a just man and did not wish to expose her to the ordeal of public disgrace; therefore, he resolved to divorce her quietly."

When I read of Joseph's fidelity to the law, I am reminded of the importance of being a just person. Do I practice justice in my interactions and relationships? There is always room for improvement. Perhaps I offer a prayer to St. Joseph invoking his intercession. I identify with the biblical character, or in Ignatian terminology, "consider the person." I may even expand my dialogue with God and others to include the biblical character I am considering, in this case St. Joseph. "St. Joseph, help me to follow the example you set, treating others as my faith, conscience, and divine mercy require."

I encounter Joseph's unwillingness to expose Mary to public shame, which in her case as a woman caught in adultery (cf. Jn 7:53—8:11) could have resulted in a public interrogation in the Jewish courts and exposure of her misdeeds, possibly leading to stoning in accordance with the Old Testament prescriptions (cf. Deut 22). He could have subjected her to the obscure and strange test of the bitter waters, the law of the *sotah* in Jewish terminology (cf. Num 5:11-31). Such legal proceedings would have exonerated Joseph of fornication and cleared his name and reputation, if not his conscience. Instead, he opted for mercy and self-sacrifice. I am inspired by his humble selflessness and am motivated to follow suit in parallel challenges in my life.

Saving face, so important in the eastern cultures, mattered less to Joseph than preserving Mary's dignity and protecting her from public humiliation and severe punishment. He simply couldn't bring himself to sacrifice her at the altar of strict justice. He did what he could to prevent such. He anticipated James' proclamation of the triumph of mercy over judgment (cf. Jas 2:13). He is an inspiration for us as we seek to respond properly to intimate wounds and interpersonal offenses.

## What Would Jesus, Mary, and Joseph Think?

What do you think the Holy Family's opinion would be of today's legalistic approach to resolving family conflicts and other interpersonal disputes within the Christian community?

One of the most appalling, destructive, and unrecognized scandals in contemporary society is the use of the legal system to exact vengeance or disproportionate punishment on (ex)spouses, family members, or neighbors. Some form of false witness, calumny, or slander is almost inevitable in such circumstances. This is an important topic that deserves more discussion and guidance within the Church—and courage to challenge the culture.

In 1 Cor 6:1-8, St. Paul harshly chastises the Corinthians for resorting to pagan courts for disputes that could be handled within the Christian community. He observes that the accusers or plaintiffs in such proceedings are themselves also committing injustices, sometimes the very ones they are prosecuting.

Like St. Joseph, they would be better off being victimized than becoming a victimizer themselves. St. Paul in words and St. Joseph in intentions and deeds expose the dark side of strict justice in family affairs.

Each of us is called to emulate Joseph in keeping justice and mercy in a healthy tension. *Kai*, the Greek conjunction linking the two in Mt 1:19 itself reflects this tension and ambiguity, as it can be translated as "yet/but" (implying tension) or "and" (implying synchronicity or complementarity).

## We Are Called to Be Faithful, Not Successful

Like Joseph, in trying to do the right thing we are susceptible to both failure and providential interventions. Moses comes to mind in this regard. He avenged the Hebrew slave being beaten by the taskmaster, and was blackmailed by an unjust Hebrew and forced into exile (cf. Exod 2:11-14). Yet, God did not desert him, and eventually revealed He had plans for him beyond his wildest imagination.

Failure in human affairs does not necessarily mean that we are at fault. Jesus is the ultimate testimony to this. Rather, as in the case of St. Thomas More and countless other saints and martyrs, it can reveal that we are God's good servants, disposed to do His will even when it conflicts with ours.

In order to discern whether we are at fault and in need of correction we need the support and guidance of friends, family, peers, and especially the Church. One of the functions of the Sacrament of Reconciliation is to align divine and human reconciliation, thereby making the penitent and the Church whole again.

I believe that one reason St. Joseph's intercession is so universally efficacious, as articulated by St. Teresa, is his practical, lived synthesis of justice, mercy, and reconciliation. Without comprehending or presumably relishing the missions entrusted to him by the Angel, he went along and accepted it at a great personal cost as well as reward.

Was celibacy easy for Joseph, or for that matter, any members of the Holy Family? This is a question we rarely ask ourselves. Surely Joseph can relate to our personal and family difficulties from the inside, as one who has been there.

St. Joseph encourages us not to be discouraged by either our own imperfect efforts at *lectio divina* or the dryness we experience. He inspires us to continue moving forward in our journey with the Lord, as he did, walking by faith rather than by sight (cf. 2 Cor 5:7), putting one foot in front of the other, to use a favorite expression of Mother Teresa.

- *When I struggle with chastity, obedience, and fidelity, do I take consolation from the fact that the Holy Family did as well, while providing us with an accessible example for emulation?*

## Receptivity to Revelation

Joseph's integrity disposes him to receptivity to God's word. This reminds us that we should not draw an artificial distinction between our prayer and apostolic life. God can speak to us outside of our devotional and liturgical activities, and we should keep our eyes and ears open to His initiative.

God only called out to Moses in the desert after He noticed him making the long and potentially treacherous journey to investigate the burning bush (cf. Exod 3:4). Moses' years in the desert hadn't robbed him of his curiosity and initiative. If anything, it seems to have tempered and refined him.

Likewise we have our desert periods where without our even noticing it God works on us, molding us into the person we are meant to be. *Lectio divina* helps us to listen, discern, and be responsive to God's transformational initiatives, even when we don't consciously perceive or understand them.

Moses' encounter with God was not a passive one. He had to take steps in God's direction for God's providential response to go to the next level. The burning bush was a divine sign that Moses chose to respond to. Similarly, the Angel's message was a sign to Joseph of God's will for his life.

Like Moses and Joseph we are called to respond faithfully to God's word and initiative, regardless of whether it seems to be in our best interests. Hopefully we contemplate and cooperate rather than calculate and manipulate. Our response will be imperfect, but we can be consoled by the realization that with God, intentions and efforts are what count. Human beings judge by appearance, but God reads our hearts (cf. 1 Sam 16:7).

## Living *Lectio*

In a certain sense Joseph lived *lectio*, even prior to unconsciously receiving God's word. A life of integrity is a firm foundation for cooperating with God's word. John the Baptist also models this in his life, ministry, and message. Immorality impedes our ability to hear and respond to God's word.

Joseph's struggle to be just, merciful, and self-sacrificing (by allowing his honor and reputation to suffer along with Mary's) reveals that he tried to do God's will instinctively, even without external prompting. However, he is humble, flexible, and obedient enough to change his course at the angelic prompting. God and life offer us many opportunities to emulate Joseph, if only we are willing to read the divine and human signs of the times and our lives.

## Holistic Fidelity

Given his receptivity to the divine revelations communicated through dreams, we can say that Joseph's fidelity extends to the unconscious level as well. We are reminded that we need to be good stewards of our subconscious mind, avoiding destructive messages by monitoring our cultural intake and keeping ourselves unstained by the world (cf. Jas 1:27; Rom 12:2).

As discussed previously, *lectio divina* can be a form of divine therapy, affecting the conscious and subconscious mind as well as our emotions, spirit, identity, and relationships. When we expose ourselves to the healing and transformational potentialities of God's word, we gradually dislodge the negative, disabling messages received in childhood and reinforced in adult life, and replace them with positive divine and human input. Formed by God's word at all levels of our being, we are better able to fulfill the two great commandments, to love God with our whole selves and our neighbor as ourselves.

## The Levels of Meaning in Scripture

In practicing *lectio*, we gradually become aware of the different levels of meaning in Scripture. As discussed in chapter one, there are several paradigms of these levels in Jewish and Christian tradition, but my favorite is the Jewish *pardes* (a Persian word meaning paradise or orchard) model, because it serves as a mnemonic acronym. *Pardes'* levels are:

- literal / historical / straightforward (*peshat*)
- allegorical / symbolic (*remez*)
- midrashic / applied / homiletic (*derash*)
- mystical / for those graced by God with infused contemplation (*sod*)

The most famous Jewish midrash, *"The Four Who Entered Paradise"* offers insights into the proper attitude by which we should approach God's word. Akiba ben Joseph, the sole rabbi who survived the test intact, safely ascending and descending from paradise, was renowned for his knowledge of Scripture and Jewish tradition and for his devotion to his wife who supported him in his studies and vocation. His execution by the Romans in A.D. 135 for his participation in the Bar Kokhba messianic revolt prompted this observation attributed to Moses in the Talmud, the oral legal tradition (*halakah*) codified in the Mishnah around A.D. 200 and supplemented with commentary (known as the Gemara) in the next several centuries.

After being transported to the time of Akiba, Moses asked God why He would give the Torah through him when a wonderful student and teacher like Akiba was available. God replied only "Be silent; such is my will." Moses persisted, and asked to be shown Akiba's reward, and God graphically revealed his martyrdom. Prefiguring the sober candor of St. Teresa, Moses exclaimed, "This is Your Torah, and such is Your reward?"

In their rich traditions and timeless values Judaism and Catholicism have much in common, including an understanding of the demands and injustices that accompany fidelity to God's word.

Another parallel between Jewish and Christian tradition on biblical spirituality comes to us through the twelfth century Carthusian monk, Guigo II, whose influential book *The Ladder of Monks and Twelve Meditations* helped spread the methodology of *lectio divina* in the middle ages. Reminiscent of the *pardes* midrash, he uses vertical images such as ladder and rungs to describe the progressive movement in *lectio divina*.

## The Flexibility of *Lectio Divina*

*Lectio divina* is a flexible model of the process human beings undergo in response to significant human or divine stimulus, in theological language, signs, and in particular the word of God. These progressive and methodical constructs are meant as guidelines or models rather than blueprints. We should not interpret the stages of either *lectio divina* or *pardes* as rigidly linear or mechanical. We can oscillate between them according to the movement of the Spirit and our natural interaction with the source text given our present circumstances, tendencies, and capacities.

We should also not assign a moral or developmental hierarchy to these levels, as if the person who focuses on the literal or applied meaning or action stage is somehow less holy or spiritual than the contemplative person who derives a mystical meaning from the text. Each level and activity is a subjective process that does not grant us immunity from error. We are susceptible to misinterpretation and self-delusion in encountering the Scriptures at any point, particularly when we lack either the requisite technical background or humility. Thus *Dei Verbum* (section 25) closes with this admonition to the faithful that recalls the teaching of one of the pioneers of biblical spirituality in the early church, St. Ambrose: "Therefore, they should gladly put themselves in touch with the sacred text itself, whether it be through the liturgy, rich in the divine word, or through devotional reading, or through instructions suitable for the purpose and other aids which, in our time, with approval and active support of the shepherds of the Church, are commendably spread everywhere. And let them remember that prayer should accompany the reading of Sacred Scripture, so that God and man may talk together; for 'we speak to Him when we pray; we hear Him when we read the divine saying.' "

The Council Fathers recognized the multiple forums through which we can encounter the Bible, beginning with the liturgy and including both *lectio divina* or spiritual reading and spirituality and study aids. I have found papal documents along with good biblical spirituality books such as those by Cardinal Martini, Fr. Demetrius Dumm, and Fr. Donald X. Burt to be rich in insights into the biblical text and good fodder for *lectio divina*. They help me stay in touch with the literal sense while deducing my personal applications.

Our susceptibility to misunderstandings and misguided interpretations and applications is exacerbated when we ambitiously seek mystical meanings rather than humbly let them be revealed to us. Pride, naiveté, immaturity, and lack of self-knowledge can distort our perspective. Both the Church and mainstream Jewish tradition have always cautioned against an inordinate inclination towards mystical interpretation, particularly at the expense of a more literal understanding and practical response. As Pope Pius XII emphasized in his landmark 1943 encyclical, *Divino Afflante Spiritu* ("On Promoting Biblical Studies"), the literal sense is the basis for all the other levels of meaning in the Bible—and we might extrapolate, in life as well. Otherwise subjectivity would dominate and we could too easily manipulate the meaning of the text or a life experience or communication in accordance with our bias and agenda.

This background is offered as a reminder to take into account the historical background and Jewish context of the Scriptures. This is particularly true in Matthew, Romans, Galatians, Hebrews, James, and Revelation, which are so obviously rooted in Old Testament imagery and themes.

## God's Communication Mode to Joseph

In reading the first two chapters of Matthew, we take note of a pattern of divine communication: God speaks to Joseph in dreams. Joseph, the guardian of Jesus, shares his name with Israel's guardian, Joseph, son of Jacob, whose dreams initially get him into trouble with his brothers but later help him find favor with Pharaoh. Jacob also experienced dreams that brought him closer to God, though not without a struggle. St. Joseph likewise experienced his dreams as a challenge as well as a blessing.

The great artists of the Renaissance and the Baroque period often brought out the difficult consequences of Joseph's obedience to the revelations he received in his dreams. My favorite painting of this genre is "The Dream of Joseph" (1773) by the German master Anton Raphael Mengs. It graces the cover of this book. The painting is located in the Ringling Museum (Sarasota, Florida), which has one of the finest Renaissance and Baroque collections in the United States.

Each mission Joseph received was fraught with unanswered questions, risks, and perils. Like Abraham, Joseph went obediently into the unknown (cf. Gen 12:4). Similarly, we are invited on a difficult journey, with *lectio divina* as a compass and the Spirit and the Church as our guide and companion. As Cardinal Martini has pointed out: "God does not speak to Joseph in dreams in order to entertain or impress him. In the mind of Matthew they point towards the Old Testament dreamers and events (e.g., Pharaoh's slaughter of the Hebrew children as a precursor of Herod's infanticide) while also announcing the new era inaugurated by the incarnation. The infancy narrative in Matthew is often referred to as a proleptic passion narrative because it introduces themes that will be revisited during Jesus' ministry and particularly during his passion and death."

## The Timelessness of the Scriptures

In the suffering endured by the Holy Family, the suffering of believers of all eras is anticipated. The persecution, arduous travel, temporary homelessness (refugee experience), and reputation damage (from Mary's miraculous pregnancy) are crosses that in various forms we must also bear. We can take consolation in the fact that even the Holy Family was not spared them. It follows that they are efficacious advocates and intercessors.

Many persons in our midst, perhaps including ourselves, undergo gut-wrenching trials similar to those of the Holy Family. Scripture is an existential, living document like no other—its drama is played out repeatedly in our lives as salvation history continues to unfold. God wants all persons to be saved (cf. 1 Tim 2:4; 2 Pet 3:9). He remains actively involved in human and personal history (cf. Mt 28:20). Through *lectio divina*, we can engage God and the communion of saints, along with our contemporary brothers and sisters, in spirited dialogue, and experience God's consoling presence and support. Where two or more are gathered in Jesus' name, He is in their midst (cf. Mt 18:15).

## Personalizing the Scriptures

Because Matthew's infancy narrative focuses on Joseph, I spend part of my *lectio* time on him, thereby respecting the literal meaning of the text, the author's apparent meaning. In order to personalize it, I try to identify with Joseph's struggle. Because Scripture is very sparing with details as to what is going on inside a person, it is up to me to fill in the blanks, especially with regards to my own experience, perspective, and reaction. In this way I participate in the passage and identify and wrestle with the key points and persons.

I take time to consider Joseph's situation and perspective, without dramatizing, rationalizing, or psychologizing it (stripping it of its moral and spiritual values). I come to the conclusion that his primary feeling must have been disappointment. Whether he felt betrayed is another matter. Throughout the centuries the saints have come to different conclusions as to Joseph's state of mind.

Sometimes it is helpful, whether during or outside of our *lectio* time, to consult a biblical commentary in order to gain another perspective or clarify a confusing passage. This enables us to read the Scriptures within the context of the Catholic tradition and community.

This helps us avoid the error of private interpretation, which involves treating our interpretations independently as dogma by implicitly assigning ourselves an inerrancy properly attributed to the Holy Spirit. This inherently places us in opposition to fellow believers and the Church as a whole.

## Consider the Person: Identifying with Joseph

St. Francis de Sales' comments in *Introduction to the Devout Life* are particularly instructive and inspirational regarding the non-judgmental attitude we should have towards others. St. Francis infers that as a just and merciful man, Joseph would leave Mary's moral culpability to God and give her the benefit of the doubt. Jesus is often portrayed as giving the benefit of the doubt to others during His ministry. Do I do the same in my interactions, particularly with family and friends, with whom familiarity and resentment can dull my sensibilities and objectivity?

## Joseph's Interior Dilemma

The phrase that comes to my mind with regard to Joseph is that he must have "collapsed interiorly," that is, experienced profound inner turmoil. He didn't know what to think or do, but he knew he had to make a decision and act. He didn't have a satisfactory choice available. We can identify with that. Sometimes there doesn't seem to be an adequate resolution to a problem, and we simply have to come up with our best decision and response. I can turn to St. Joseph for guidance and consolation when faced with such situations.

In *lectio* we should not only consider the human persons, but pre-eminently, the divine. Why would God put Joseph and Mary in such a situation? They were completely innocent, yet they would be seen by society as guilty no matter how Joseph resolved it. Again, we are reminded never to judge by appearances. The New Testament speaks of this often (cf. 1 Cor 4:4-5; Rom 2:1-4; Jas 2:1-4; Heb 10:38).

## The Test of Timing

God allowed Joseph to undergo excruciating inner turmoil before finally providing a way out at the last minute. I often experience a solution being provided (God coming to the rescue) in seemingly hopeless situations only at the last minute, like the Angel when Abraham is ready to slay his son. God's timing seems like a test. With Moses, Jeremiah, and Job as inspiration, I cry, "test someone else."

Reflection on Joseph's quandary leads me to consider the timing of the respective annunciations. Without becoming overly analytical and imposing modern logic and curiosity on ancient literature, it seems reasonable to presume that Mary either received the message of the Angel before Joseph did, or concurrently, and hadn't yet told him. Perhaps she hadn't had the chance or didn't know how to broach the subject. Some mysteries are beyond words. Mary and Joseph know the awkwardness and misunderstandings couples undergo from firsthand experience.

The text's ambiguity cautions us against exaggerated emphasis on details or imaginative speculation at the same time that it invites responsible reflection and application to our life. We might consider awkward and perplexing circumstances in our life in which communications become confusing or upsetting, even when the parties involved have sincere intentions. We can *lectio* on these texts and invite the Holy Family's intercession while trying to emulate their honorable behavior.

Scripture's silence invites our reverent reflection and deductions, not merely in the abstract, but concretely, as it relates to our circumstances and in particular our relationship with God, self, and others.

Recognizing that biblical characters, including Jesus, Mary, and Joseph were not immune to confusion, misunderstandings, intense mental, emotional, and spiritual suffering, and mysterious divine testing, I don't view such necessarily as punishment, but rather as an invitation to share in the suffering of Jesus and His body, the Church (cf. Col 1:24). We become bound with them in an intimate and purifying way.

*Lectio* thereby becomes an occasion for our participation in the ongoing dialogue of salvation, which is punctuated with suffering as well as joy. *Lectio* then moves from being simply a devotional process to a dialogue and lifestyle orientation led by the Spirit in union with the Church.

Thus whenever I am confronted with the harsh realities of life, including feelings of disappointment in and alienation from God, I can turn first and foremost to Jesus, but also to Mary and Joseph for hope and consolation.

- *What lessons and personal applications and parallels can I derive from the Holy Family's mysterious, awkward, and painful beginning?*
- *What dilemmas in my life are brought to mind, and how do these texts and my prayerful reflections shed light on the appropriate response?*

## Humanizing the Scriptures

To humanize the Scriptures is to recognize the core human values, needs, and problems that they showcase, and their timelessness and personal relevance. We can then accept the Spirit's invitation to become part of the text, to discover how the biblical drama continues to be played out in history as well as in our lives. As discussed in chapter two, this requires discernment, a spiritual practice and art that includes becoming sensitive to the divine and human signs in our lives. The word we engage in *lectio divina* can be a divine or human sign for us.

The Bible, and especially the biblical characters, can become real, familiar, and increasingly central to our life. We recognize that God continues to reveal Himself in the pages of our lives. As Mother Teresa often observed, we become the pencil through which God writes, His hands and feet. The events, values, challenges, and characters of the Bible are repeated in our individual and communal lives, if only we will open our eyes and hearts and read the signs of our times and lives.

Recognizing this enables me to humanize and personalize the Bible and receive it as a dialogical invitation from God to accept my role in salvation history. I can only do so properly through fidelity to the Spirit and the Church. It can be easy to love God, but loving our neighbor and the imperfect guides, companions, and authorities He places in our lives and history is another matter. *Lectio*, privately, communally, liturgically, and sacramentally, can help us work towards such obedient responsiveness (cf. Eph 5:31).

*Lectio divina* is an opportunity to recognize and assume the role God is offering us in the divine and human drama; we accept the gifts and possibilities He shares along with the awesome responsibilities and challenges. Joseph and Mary are pivotal characters in our struggle to bring the Bible to life because the challenges they faced bridged humanity and divinity, reaching the highest expression in their son, Jesus.

- *In what ways can I relate to Joseph and Mary?*
- *What experiences and challenges do I share with them?*

## Joseph, Matthew's Model Believer

Matthew portrays Joseph as the faithful Israelite and disciple who more than any other character in the Gospel explicitly fulfills the judgment criteria in the eschatological (end times) parable of the sheep and the goats (cf. Mt 25:31-46). The elect are humble, just, and merciful, bringing to mind the first believer in Matthew's Gospel, Joseph, who unassumingly welcomed Jesus and Mary at their most vulnerable points. Is it any wonder that St. Teresa assures us of his heavenly influence and support?

Matthew desires to show Jesus as the fulfillment of the Old Testament and thereby nourish the faith of his Jewish Christian community. Joseph brings to life the fundamental values of Matthew's Gospel: justice, obedience, perseverance, suffering, compassion, chastity, mercy, and humility, each of which is firmly rooted in the Old Testament.

Reflecting on Joseph and on Matthew's Gospel gives us the opportunity to rediscover the Hebrew roots of our faith and experience the Bible as its original audience did. Through the principle of reminiscence, we can link Old and New Testament passages and discover how they have been fulfilled in Jesus and are primed for further fulfillment in our lives, through the life of the Spirit. In 2001, the Pontifical Biblical Commission published an informative and erudite document on the subject, "The Jewish People and Their Sacred Scriptures in the Christian Bible." It is available on the Vatican website, www.vatican.va.

One of the principles I discussed in chapter four of The *St. Joseph Guide to the Bible* was how to interpret the Bible contextually. Given its length, breadth, and foundational nature, the Old Testament is a significant part of this context. The axiom "The Bible interprets itself" means that we understand individual Bible passages through reference to related passages and the Bible's message as a whole. It does not imply that the Bible is self-explanatory nor that it frees us from the hermeneutical (the science of interpretation, a scholarly term for exegetical) challenge.

## Gender Differences and Dignity Illuminated in the Bible

We notice that in contrast to texts relating to Joseph, Mary's encounter with an Angel is a fully conscious one. In the Bible, most revelations in dreams are directed to men; women tend to encounter God more on a conscious level. A prominent Matthean exception is Pilate's wife, and he ignored her warning (cf. Mt 27:19).

When I reflect on the unconscious nature of Joseph's revelatory encounters, I am reminded of the primordial one, described in the book of Genesis, whereby Eve is created from Adam's side / rib while he is asleep. In his "Theology of the Body" talks, Pope John Paul II acknowledges the significant role of the subconscious mind in referring to what depth psychologists such as Carl Jung have taught us. In both Adam's and Joseph's cases, the mysteries they are being introduced to are almost too good to be true, constituting authentic reasons for rejoicing, though down the road they will also be the cause of trials and difficulties.

## Stewardship of the Unconscious Mind through *Lectio*

When as part of the meditation stage we repeat our word and internalize it, we engage it on a subconscious level and thereby bring inspired input to an aspect of our being that is often overlooked, despite being exposed to many unsavory conditionings. Fr. Thomas Keating refers to the dynamic that occurs during contemplative prayer as the "unloading of the unconscious" and "divine therapy." We replace our negative internal messages (often received early in life or at significant points in adolescence and adulthood) with authentic, affirming messages and directives gleaned from God's word. We are responsible for stewardship of our subconscious mind along with the rest of our faculties.

In summary, Joseph's conscious and subconscious receptivity to revelation remind us that we need to bring our whole selves to the *lectio* process, which itself is inherently holistic. In so doing, we take small steps toward fulfilling the commandments of holistic love of God, self, and neighbor.

## Gender Dimensions of Inspiration

When I reflect on the unconscious dimension of Joseph's encounters with the Angel, I recall both my own dreams and the spiritual significance I accorded them, and the deep, gut level resonance of God's spirit within me in certain instances. For example, in finding the girl of my dreams, making a major decision, or undergoing a life-changing experience. Something runs so deep in me as to be almost uncommunicable. I recall Adam's poetic eloquence marked by repetitive non-descriptive vocabulary—three times he refers to his new counterpart as this (one)—in announcing the fulfillment of his dreams, Eve. Anticipating the tongue-tied state of men throughout history when first encountering the woman of their dreams, he cannot find the words to describe her.

I often remark to attendees at my gender relations or theology of the body presentations that we often find the deepest cultural or aesthetic expressions offered by men who are inspired by women. A woman can be so supportive and loving that her male admirer is moved to dig deep into his untapped potential and arrive at creative expressions and appreciative actions in response.

Conversely, a woman who purposefully acts as an impediment to a man can very easily bring him down in one way or another. The fulfillment of a man's vocation and potential is significantly influenced by the women in his life, perhaps even more so than the other way around. The Old Testament wisdom literature speaks often of these positive and negative dimensions of female influence.

Returning to the literal meaning and context of the text, I am reminded that Joseph's dreams refer to something near and dear to the heart of most men: the love of their life and their children. I recall Fr. Theodore M. Hesburgh's classic observation that the most important thing a father can do for his children is to love their mother. I believe this to be true on every level: spiritual, moral, psychological, sociological, and developmental.

Thus when I read of Joseph's unwillingness to humiliate his wife even when apparently she has done him a great injustice, I experience in the depths of my being a profound resonance, not primarily at the level of abstraction, but as a matter of will and principle. Call it the protective dimension of masculinity, perhaps, or impute any other meaning to it that you wish, but I know instinctively that to preserve a wife's honor is one of a husband's most sacred duties, or better, privileges.

When I read about St. Joseph's honorable intentions, and the price that he was willing to pay, I am inspired to live that way and accept the consequences. I never tire of reflecting on St. Joseph's response to this inconceivable, gut-wrenching dilemma, because emulating him never becomes easy or mundane. Egocentric vindication is sweet initially but eventually sours and poisons.

Women can consider reciprocal principles relevant to their life and vocation. There is always a human and personal as well as gender element in the text.

- *Am I respectful of my loved one's reputation, avoiding exposing them to public humiliation if at all possible?*
- *Am I willing to sacrifice for and suffer with my loved one?*
- *Do I keep in mind and respect the dignity of the opposite sex and their right to be regarded with appreciation and consideration? Are my attitudes and actions consistent with this? What small steps might I take to love, serve, and reach out to them better?*

## Dealing with Dryness and Discouragement

God's word was cultivated in Mary and Joseph in unrepeatable ways precisely because they proved to be fertile ground for

God's communications and will amid disconcerting circumstances. Thus whenever I do *lectio* and don't feel that I am getting anything out of it, my recognition that God works in His own time and way consoles me and compels me to persist in my *lectio* despite the apparent dryness. I may not see the fruits of my *lectio* right away, but down the road, perhaps when I least expect it, God can reveal to me the deeper meaning of a passage I initially only skimmed the surface of.

We are like sponges in which the water seeps through only gradually. In *lectio*, we soak up God's word and become repositories of it. Pope Benedict uses water imagery with reference to *lectio*, as follows:

"Among the many fruits of this *biblical springtime* I would like to mention the spread of the ancient practice of *Lectio divina* or 'spiritual reading' of Sacred Scripture. It consists in pouring over a biblical text for some time, reading it and rereading it, as it were, 'ruminating' on it as the Fathers say and squeezing from it, so to speak, all its 'juice,' so that it may nourish meditation and contemplation and, *like water*, succeed in *irrigating life itself"* (Benedict XVI, November 6, 2005).

In my presentations, I often reference Benedict's ringing prophetic phrase with respect to a revival of *lectio divina*, "a new spiritual spring," recognizing both senses of the word "spring" because *lectio* emulates water's life-giving qualities and is regenerative, as spring is in the seasons of nature. The word of God is fertile. The question is, what kind of soil are we? Agricultural imagery and themes permeate the parables, lending themselves to powerful metaphors that we can ponder in relation to our lives.

## Pregnant Passages

The passage which describes Mary's heretofore unexplained conception is remarkable for its profound brevity and pregnant meaning, no pun intended. Like much of the Bible, it is waiting to burst forth with possibilities because it addresses fundamental issues whose variety and depth of meaning can never be exhausted. It reminds us that we don't need a large chunk of Scripture in order to find a word that speaks to us. True, sometimes we must read awhile before we encounter the word meant for us and our comprehension. Signs can be slow in coming. Other times the profundity and personal attractiveness of a particular passage makes extended reading unnecessary. We are thrust into the intimate gaze of God and accept His invitation to rest in Him, for His yoke is easy and His burden light.

However, the efficacy of our *lectio* is not a matter of feelings or insights, but responsiveness. Joseph reminds us of this. He says nothing. Scripture is similarly silent about the details of his life, informing us only of his lineage, domain, and profession. Nonetheless, Joseph models many of the qualities (e.g., humility, obedience, mercy, compassion, integrity, justice, courage, and self-discipline) that can make our *lectio* a dynamic, lived experience. He also reminds us that God can speak to us at any time and in different and demanding ways.

As I reflect on this brief but powerful passage in the Bible, and find myself having difficulty being succinct, I am reminded of the Bible's endless possibilities. Every time we come to the Bible we are capable of learning something new, or of being transformed and renewed. As discussed in chapter one, God's word is dynamic and efficacious. Grace and divine providence cannot be exhausted. They can only be blunted by our intransigence—in biblical terms, hard-heartedness, i.e., resistance to God's word and will.

So far, we have focused on Joseph's original dilemma and the Angel's annunciation to him. A comprehensive reflection on the infancy narratives is beyond our scope. We'll conclude with a brief reflection on the ensuing Holy Family adventures as related by Matthew (which have parallels in the so-called "Joseph cycle" in Genesis 37—50), focusing on their implications for our understanding of Joseph and *lectio*, this book's models. Using the *lectio* lens, let's review and summarize the subsequent dream revelations and their individual and cumulative meanings.

## Dream On

In Matthew's Gospel Joseph does not hold a monopoly on revelatory dreams. The magi are informed of Herod's bad faith in a dream, and return home via a different route. Mrs. Pilate dreams about Jesus. In subsequent dreams Joseph is instructed to leave for Egypt to flee the murderous Herod, return to Judea upon the ruler's death, and go north to Galilee to avoid Archelaus, his successor. That's a lot of traveling for a poor family with a young child in the ancient world.

The aforementioned painting in the Ringling Museum, "The Dream of Joseph" (1773) by Mengs, captures in ways words and abstractions cannot, the difficulties faithfully endured by St. Joseph. The painter captures the muscular forearm of the carpenter pressed against his chin in a futile effort to stay awake while an exquisitely soft, pale, and beautiful Angel points him gently but firmly on his way. When I gaze at that painting, I am visually convicted of Joseph's noble masculine care for the Holy Family and reminded that fidelity to the word of God is not an abstraction but an incarnate reality constituted by obedience in concrete ways and circumstances.

In simultaneously obeying Jesus, *The* Word of God, and receiving His obedience, together with his spouse, the Virgin of Nazareth, St. Joseph constitutes an unsurpassed model of receptivity, virtue, and perseverance that can inspire us as we follow in their footsteps. May our *lectio* ever be an occasion of hearing and doing the word of God as we encounter it and Him in our daily lives, mindful of the support available to us in the family of God, beginning with Jesus, Mary, and Joseph.

We could best honor Joseph first by following and drawing strength from his family's example, and second by frequently reciting, and doing *lectio* on the biblical prayers given us in memory of his loved ones, the Hail Mary and the Lord's Prayer.

# Popescript

BECAUSE of all the applications and dimensions associated with *lectio divina*, it is easy to forget that its primary function is to facilitate a personal encounter with God. That may also be its most difficult aspect. It is easy, though less fulfilling, to delude ourselves and relate to God on a superficial level, keeping things comfortable and ordered according to our agenda. We thereby invert the moral and religious order, acting as if we are in charge and failing to entrust ourselves to divine providence.

Because self-delusion is an ever-present temptation, it is important to have a spiritual director, confessor, confidant, or support group to recognize disparities and offer encouragement, correction, and (re)direction.

I refer to this addendum as a popescript because Pope Benedict has frequently emphasized the dangers of an overly rationalistic and speculative approach to Scripture by scholars. This is also a temptation for non-specialists. We can keep Scripture in our head and isolate it from our heart. This dilutes our experience of *lectio divina* and impedes closeness with God. Jesus' farewell discourse in the Gospel of John, chapters 14—17, proclaims the intimacy the Trinity offers as the fruit of our obedience to Christ's commandment ("love one another as I have loved you").

We need not become uptight or scrupulous about this. *Lectio divina*, like life, can't be scripted or rigidly controlled. God understands our weakness and desires, and does not expect perfection. He can write straight with crooked lines, provided that our intentions are good. We should take a positive, hopeful approach, remembering that *lectio divina* is an invitation to intimacy and is something to treasure and cultivate rather than tolerate, dread, or be anxious or ambivalent about. Like anything worthwhile, it is not easy.

The dialogical motif we have emphasized helps us relate personally to God during *lectio divina*. Otherwise we are tempted to analyze, rationalize, idealize, and mull over things from a distance. The indispensable ingredient is silence; the operative virtues are humility, obedience, and perseverance. The fruits are those of the Spirit, articulated by St. Paul in Gal 5:22. Look them up, reflect on them in the context of the passage and your life, and invite the Spirit to produce them within you.

I find the writings of Thomas Merton (1915-1968) particularly helpful with respect to the contemplative, catechetical, and evangelical dimensions of *lectio divina*. He offers many practical guidelines and insights born not only of his own personal and pastoral experience, but also of his familiarity with the lives and writings of the saints, especially the mystics. He is eloquent, straightforward, realistic, and balanced. We often get the impression he is writing about us.

Our reticence to relate intimately to God can be rooted in emotional and spiritual wounds, particularly major disappointments, losses, and relationship difficulties or break-ups. We can bring these to prayer as part of the *lectio divina* process and thereby dispose ourselves to divine healing.

Just as in a conversation with a loved one we need leeway to be candid and spontaneous, so with God anything in our life is fair game for dialogue. Our freedom and candor is enhanced by the realization that we don't have to worry about His sensitivities the way we do our neighbor's. We can let it all hang out without impunity, and become closer to God, ourselves, and others in the process.

I have been writing and speaking on *lectio divina* for over twenty years, yet still struggle to open myself fully to God's healing touch. As with any therapy, pain is usually a prelude and accompaniment to joy and renewal (cf. Jn 16:20-22; Isa 43:18-19; Rev 21:5).

Lord, may my *lectio divina* never become simply a religious practice or ideological head game.

May I let the word of God form me, rather than manipulate it for my own purposes, heaven forbid at the expense of others.

May I embrace the silence God invites me to and bask in His presence, regardless of whether I experience any feelings or sensations of such.

May I persevere, knowing how this pleases Him. Amen.

# Bibliography

## *Lectio Divina*

*Christian Prayer*, the official one-volume edition of the *Liturgy of the Hours*, with complete texts of Morning and Evening Prayer for the year. Totowa, NJ: Catholic Book Publishing Corp., 1976.

*Shorter Christian Prayer*, with Morning and Evening Prayer from the Four-Week Psalter and selected texts for the Seasons and Major Feasts of the year. A user-friendly, portable version of the above. Totowa, NJ: Catholic Book Publishing Corp., 1988.

Binz, Stephen J. *Conversing with God in Scripture: A Contemporary Approach to* Lectio Divina. Ijamsville, MD: The Word Among Us Press, 2008.

Casey, Michael. *Sacred Reading: The Ancient Art of* Lectio Divina. Liguori, MO: Liguori/Triumph, 1995.

Guigo II. *The Ladder of Monks and Twelve Meditations.* Translated by Edmund Colledge and James Walsh. Kalamazoo, MI: Cistercian Publications, 1981. (Classic medieval work on *lectio*.)

Hall, Thelma. *Too Deep for Words: Rediscovering* Lectio Divina. Mahwah, NJ: Paulist Press, 1988.

Leclercq, Dom Jean. *The Love of Learning and the Desire for God.* New York: Mentor Omega Books, 1962. (Classic modern work on *lectio divina*.)

Magrassi, Mariano. *Praying the Bible: An Introduction to* Lectio Divina. Collegeville, MN: The Liturgical Press, 1998.

Masini, Mario. Lectio Divina: *An Ancient Prayer That Is Ever New.* Staten Island, NY: Alba House, 1998.

Pennington, M. Basil. Lectio Divina: *Renewing the Ancient Practice of Praying the Scriptures.* New York: The Crossroad Publishing Company, 1998.

## Works by the Author

Schultz, Karl A. *The Art and Vocation of Caring for Persons in Pain.* Mahwah, NJ: Paulist Press, 1994.

——. *Bearing the Unbearable: Coping with Infertility and Other Profound Suffering.* Ann Arbor, MI: Nimble Books, 2007.

——. *Becoming Community.* New York: New City Press, 2007.

——. *Calming the Stormy Seas of Stress.* Winona, MN: St. Mary's Press, 1998.

——. *The How-To Book of the Bible.* Huntington, IN: Our Sunday Visitor, 2004.

——. *How to Pray with the Bible: The Ancient Prayer Form of* Lectio Divina *Made Simple.* Huntington, IN: Our Sunday Visitor, 2007.

——. *Job Therapy.* Pittsburgh, PA: Genesis Personal Development Center, 1996.

——. *Journaling with Moses and Job.* Boston: Pauline Books & Media, 1996.

——. *Nourished by the Word: A Dialogue with Brother Andrew Campbell, O.S.B. on Praying the Scriptures and Holistic Personal Growth.* Notre Dame, IN: Ave Maria Press, 1994.

——. *Personal Energy Management: A Christian Personal and Professional Development Program.* Chicago: Loyola University Press, 1994.

——. *Personal Energy Manager Rainbow Planner.* Pittsburgh, PA: Genesis Personal Development Center, 1997.

——. *Pope Paul VI: Christian Virtues and Values.* New York: Crossroad Publishing Company, 2007.

——. *St. Joseph Guide to the Bible: Becoming Comfortable with the Bible in Four Simple Steps.* Totowa, NJ: Catholic Book Publishing Corporation, 2008.

———. *Where Is God When You Need Him?: Sharing Stories of Suffering with Job and Jesus.* Staten Island, NY: Alba House, 1992.

Schultz, Karl A. and Lorene Hanley Duquin. *The Bible and You.* Huntington, IN: Our Sunday Visitor, 2005.

The above books and CDs, and DVDs of the author's presentations on *lectio divina* and other biblical spirituality, pastoral care, and personal growth subjects can be ordered from Genesis Personal Development Center, 3431 Gass Avenue, Pittsburgh, PA, 15212-2239. The e-mail address is karlaschultz@juno.com or mrkarleno@gmail.com, and the web site is karlaschultz.com. The phone number is (412) 766-7545. Please direct media, retreat, training, and speaking requests here also.

## About the Author

Karl A. Schultz is the director of Genesis Personal Development Center in Pittsburgh. He is one of the world's most prolific authors and speakers on *lectio divina* and its application to inner healing, pastoral care, art and culture, sexuality (including Theology of the Body), communications (dialogue), spiritual development (formation), and potential fulfillment.

Schultz has published thirteen books and one audiocassette, and has presented programs on *lectio divina*, biblical spirituality, young adult formation, Pope Paul VI and Vatican II, theology of the body, St. Joseph, men's spirituality, gender communications and conflict resolution, time and stress management, suffering, caregiving, organizational development, wellness, and potential fulfillment in church, retreat, corporate, healthcare, sports, young adult, and institutional environments throughout the world. He has been interviewed on numerous national television and radio programs, including EWTN's *Bookmark, Living His Life Abundantly, Life on the Rock,* and *EWTN Live!*

As chronicled on his website, karlaschultz.com, in 2009, he embarked on a three-month *lectio divina* speaking tour of Australia and New Zealand.

# Appendix

## THE ANCIENT ART of *LECTIO DIVINA*

Fr. Luke Dysinger, O.S.B.

## 1. THE PROCESS of *LECTIO DIVINA*

A VERY ANCIENT art, practiced at one time by all Christians, is the technique known as *lectio divina*—a slow, contemplative praying of the Scriptures which enables the Bible, the Word of God, to become a means of union with God. This ancient practice has been kept alive in the Christian monastic tradition, and is one of the precious treasures of Benedictine monastics and oblates. Together with the Liturgy and daily manual labor, time set aside in a special way for *lectio divina* enables us to discover in our daily life an underlying spiritual rhythm. Within this rhythm we discover an increasing ability to offer more of ourselves and our relationships to the Father, and to accept the embrace that God is continuously extending to us in the person of his Son Jesus Christ.

### *Lectio*—reading/listening

The art of *lectio divina* begins with cultivating the ability to listen deeply, to hear "with the ear of our hearts" as St. Benedict encourages us in the Prologue to the Rule. When we read the Scriptures we should try to imitate the prophet Elijah. We should allow ourselves to become women and men who are able to listen for the still, small voice of God (1 Kings 19:12); the "faint murmuring sound" which is God's word for us, God's voice touching our hearts. This gentle listening is an "atunement" to the presence of God in that special part of God's creation which is the Scriptures.

173

The cry of the prophets to ancient Israel was the joy-filled command to "Listen!" "Sh'ma Israel: Hear, O Israel!" In *lectio divina* we, too, heed that command and turn to the Scriptures, knowing that we must "hear"—listen—to the voice of God, which often speaks very softly. In order to hear someone speaking softly we must learn to be silent. We must learn to love silence. If we are constantly speaking or if we are surrounded with noise, we cannot hear gentle sounds. The practice of *lectio divina*, therefore, requires that we first quiet down in order to hear God's word to us. This is the first step of *lectio divina*, appropriately called *lectio*—reading.

The reading or listening which is the first step in *lectio divina* is very different from the speed reading which modern Christians apply to newspapers, books and even to the Bible. *Lectio* is reverential listening; listening both in a spirit of silence and of awe. We are listening for the still, small voice of God that will speak to us personally—not loudly, but intimately. In *lectio* we read slowly, attentively, gently listening to hear a word or phrase that is God's word for us this day.

## *Meditatio*—meditation

Once we have found a word or a passage in the Scriptures that speaks to us in a personal way, we must take it in and "ruminate" on it. The image of the ruminant animal quietly chewing its cud was used in antiquity as a symbol of the Christian pondering the Word of God. Christians have always seen a scriptural invitation to *lectio divina* in the example of the Virgin Mary "pondering in her heart" what she saw and heard of Christ (Luke 2:19). For us today these images are a reminder that we must take in the word—that is, memorize it—and while gently repeating it to ourselves, allow it to interact with our thoughts, our hopes, our memories, our desires. This is the second step or stage in *lectio divina*—*meditatio*. Through *meditatio* we allow God's word to become His word for us, a word that touches us and affects us at our deepest levels.

## *Oratio*—prayer

The third step in *lectio divina* is *oratio*—prayer: prayer understood both as dialogue with God, that is, as loving conversation with the One who has invited us into His embrace; and as consecration, prayer as the priestly offering to God of parts of ourselves that we have not previously believed God wants. In this consecration-prayer we allow the word that we have taken in and on which we are pondering to touch and change our deepest selves. Just as a priest consecrates the elements of bread and wine at the Eucharist, God invites us in *lectio divina* to hold up our most difficult and pain-filled experiences to Him, and to gently recite over them the healing word or phrase He has given us in our *lectio* and *meditatio*. In this *oratio*, this consecration-prayer, we allow our real selves to be touched and changed by the word of God.

## *Contemplatio*—contemplation

Finally, we simply rest in the presence of the One who has used His word as a means of inviting us to accept His transforming embrace. No one who has ever been in love needs to be reminded that there are moments in loving relationships when words are unnecessary. It is the same in our relationship with God. Wordless, quiet rest in the presence of the One Who loves us has a name in the Christian tradition—*contemplatio*, contemplation. Once again we practice silence, letting go of our own words; this time simply enjoying the experience of being in the presence of God.

## 2. THE UNDERLYING RHYTHM of *LECTIO DIVINA*

If we are to practice *lectio divina* effectively, we must travel back in time to an understanding that today is in danger of being almost completely lost. In the Christian past the words **action** (or practice, from the Greek *praktikos*) and **contemplation** did not describe different kinds of Christians engaging (or not engaging) in different forms of prayer and apostolates. Practice and contemplation were understood as the two poles of our underlying, ongoing spiritual rhythm: a gentle oscillation back and forth between spiritual "activity" with regard to God and "receptivity."

Practice—spiritual "activity"—referred in ancient times to our active cooperation with God's grace in rooting out vices and allowing the virtues to flourish. The direction of spiritual activity was not outward in the sense of an apostolate, but **inward**— down into the depths of the soul where the Spirit of God is constantly transforming us, refashioning us in God's image. The *active life* is thus coming to see who we truly are and allowing ourselves to be remade into what God intends us to become.

In the early monastic tradition *contemplation* was understood in two ways. First was *theoria physike*, the contemplation of God in creation—God in "the many." Second was *theologia*, the contemplation of God in Himself without images or words— God as "The One." From this perspective *lectio divina* serves as a training-ground for the contemplation of God in His creation.

In contemplation we cease from interior spiritual *doing* and learn simply to *be*, that is to rest in the presence of our loving Father. Just as we constantly move back and forth in our exterior lives between speaking and listening, between questioning and reflecting, so in our spiritual lives we must learn to enjoy the refreshment of simply *being* in God's presence, an experience that naturally alternates (if we let it!) with our spiritual *practice*.

In ancient times contemplation was not regarded as a goal to be achieved through some method of prayer, but was simply accepted with gratitude as God's recurring gift. At intervals the Lord invites us to cease from speaking so that we can simply rest in his embrace. This is the pole of our inner spiritual rhythm called contemplation.

How different this ancient understanding is from our modern approach! Instead of recognizing that we all gently oscillate back and forth between spiritual activity and receptivity, between practice and contemplation, we today tend to set contemplation before ourselves as a goal—something we imagine we can achieve through some spiritual technique. We must be willing to sacrifice our "goal-oriented" approach if we are to practice *lectio divina*, because *lectio divina* has no other goal than spending time with God through the medium of His word. The amount of time we spend in any aspect of *lectio divina*, whether it be rumination, consecration or contemplation depends on God's Spirit, not on us. *Lectio divina* teaches us to savor and delight in all the different flavors of God's presence, whether they be active or receptive modes of experiencing Him.

In *lectio divina* we offer ourselves to God; and we are people in motion. In ancient times this inner spiritual motion was described as a helix—an ascending spiral. Viewed in only two dimensions it appears as a circular motion back and forth; seen with the added dimension of time it becomes a helix, an ascending spiral by means of which we are drawn ever closer to God. The whole of our spiritual lives was viewed in this way, as a gentle oscillation between spiritual activity and receptivity by means of which God unites us ever closer to Himself. In just the same way the steps or stages of *lectio divina* represent an oscillation back and forth between these spiritual poles. In *lectio divina* we recognize our underlying spiritual rhythm and discover many different ways of experiencing God's presence—many different ways of praying.

## 3. THE PRACTICE of *LECTIO DIVINA*

### Private *Lectio Divina*

Choose a text of the Scriptures that you wish to pray. Many Christians use in their daily *lectio divina* one of the readings from the Eucharistic liturgy for the day; others prefer to slowly work through a particular book of the Bible. It makes no difference which text is chosen, as long as one has no set goal of "covering" a certain amount of text: the amount of text "covered" is in God's hands, not yours.

Place yourself in a comfortable position and allow yourself to become silent. Some Christians focus for a few moments on their breathing; others have a beloved "prayer word" or "prayer phrase" they gently recite in order to become interiorly silent. For some the practice known as "centering prayer" makes a good, brief introduction to *lectio divina*. Use whatever method is best for you and allow yourself to enjoy silence for a few moments.

Then turn to the text and read it slowly, gently. Savor each portion of the reading, constantly listening for the "still, small voice" of a word or phrase that somehow says, "I am for you today." Do not expect lightening or ecstasies. In *lectio divina* God is teaching us to listen to Him, to seek Him in silence. He does not reach out and grab us; rather, He softly, gently invites us ever more deeply into His presence.

Next take the word or phrase into yourself. Memorize it and slowly repeat it to yourself, allowing it to interact with your inner world of concerns, memories and ideas. Do not be afraid of "distractions." Memories or thoughts are simply parts of yourself which, when they rise up during *lectio divina*, are asking to be given to God along with the rest of your inner self. Allow this inner pondering, this rumination, to invite you into dialogue with God.

Then, speak to God. Whether you use words or ideas or images or all three is not important. Interact with God as you would with one who you know loves and accepts you. And give to Him what you have discovered in yourself during your experience of *meditatio*. Experience yourself as the priest that you are. Experience God using the word or phrase that He has given you as a means of blessing, of transforming the ideas and memories, which your pondering on His word has awakened. Give to God what you have found within your heart.

Finally, simply rest in God's embrace. And when He invites you to return to your pondering of His word or to your inner dialogue with Him, do so. Learn to use words when words are helpful, and to let go of words when they no longer are necessary. Rejoice in the knowledge that God is with you in both words and silence, in spiritual activity and inner receptivity.

Sometimes in *lectio divina* one will return several times to the printed text, either to savor the literary context of the word or phrase that God has given, or to seek a new word or phrase to ponder. At other times only a single word or phrase will fill the whole time set aside for *lectio divina*. It is not necessary to anxiously assess the quality of one's *lectio divina* as if one were "performing" or seeking some goal: *lectio divina* has no goal other than that of being in the presence of God by praying the Scriptures.

## *Lectio Divina* as a Group Exercise

The most authentic and traditional form of Christian *lectio divina* is the solitary or "private" practice described to this point. In recent years, however, many different forms of so-called "group lectio" have become popular and are now widely practiced. These group exercises can be very useful means of introducing and encouraging the practice of *lectio divina*; but they should not become a substitute for an encounter and communion with the Living God that can only take place in that privileged solitude where the biblical Word of God becomes transparent to the Very Word Himself—namely private *lectio divina*.

In churches of the Third World where books are rare, a form of corporate *lectio divina* is becoming common in which a text from the Scriptures is pondered by Christians praying together in a group. The method of group *lectio divina* described here was introduced at St. Andrew's Abbey by oblates Doug and Norvene Vest: it is used as part of the Benedictine Spirituality for Laity workshops conducted at the Abbey each summer.

This form of *lectio divina* works best in a group of between four and eight people. A group leader coordinates the process and facilitates sharing. The same text from the Scriptures is read out three times, followed each time by a period of silence and an opportunity for each member of the group to share the fruit of her or his *lectio*.

The first reading (the text is actually read twice on this occasion) is for the purpose of hearing a word or passage that touches the heart. When the word or phrase is found, it is silently taken in, and gently recited and pondered during the silence which follows. After the silence each person shares which word or phrase has touched his or her heart.

The second reading (by a member of the opposite sex from the first reader) is for the purpose of "hearing" or "seeing" Christ in the text. Each ponders the word that has touched the heart and asks where the word or phrase touches his or her life that day. In other words, how is Christ the Word touching his own experience, his own life? How are the various members of the group seeing or hearing Christ reach out to them through the text? Then, after the silence, each member of the group shares what he or she has "heard" or "seen."

The third and final reading is for the purpose of experiencing Christ "calling us forth" into *doing* or *being*. Members ask themselves what Christ in the text is calling them to *do* or to *become* today or this week. After the silence, each shares for the last time; and the exercise concludes with each person praying for the person on the right.

Those who regularly practice this method of praying and sharing the Scriptures regularly find it to be an excellent way of developing trust within a group; it also is an excellent way of consecrating projects and hopes to Christ before more formal group meetings. A summary of this method for group *lectio divina* is appended at the end of this article.

## *Lectio Divina* on Life

In the ancient tradition *lectio divina* was understood as being one of the most important ways in which Christians experience God in creation. After all, the Scriptures are part of creation! If one is daily growing in the art of finding Christ in the pages of the Bible, one naturally begins to discover Him more clearly in aspects of the other things He has made. This includes, of course, our own personal history.

Our own lives are fit matter for *lectio divina.* Very often our concerns, our relationships, our hopes and aspirations naturally intertwine with our pondering on the Scriptures, as has been described above. But sometimes it is fitting to simply sit down and "read" the experiences of the last few days or weeks in our hearts, much as we might slowly read and savor the words of Scripture in *lectio divina.* We can attend "with the ear of our hearts" to our own memories, listening for God's gentle presence in the events of our lives. We thus allow ourselves the joy of experiencing Christ reaching out to us through our own memories. Our own personal story becomes "salvation history."

For those who are new to the practice of *lectio divina,* a group experience of "*lectio* on life" can provide a helpful introduction. An approach that has been used at workshops at St. Andrew's Priory is detailed at the end of this article. Like the experience of *lectio divina* shared in community, this group experience of *lectio* on life can foster relationships in community and enable personal experiences to be consecrated—offered to Christ—in a concrete way.

However, unlike scriptural *lectio divina* shared in community, this group *lectio* on life contains more silence than sharing. The role of group facilitators or leaders is important, since they will be guiding the group through several periods of silence and reflection without the "interruption" of individual sharing until the end of the exercise. Since the experiences we choose to "read" or "listen to" may be intensely personal, it is important in this group exercise to safeguard privacy by making sharing completely optional.

In brief, one begins with restful silence, then gently reviews the events of a given period of time. One seeks an event, a memory, which touches the heart just as a word or phrase in scriptural *lectio divina* does. One then recalls the setting, the circumstances; one seeks to discover how God seemed to be present or absent from the experience. One then offers the event to God and rests for a time in silence. A suggested method for group *lectio divina* on life is given in the Appendix to this article.

# CONCLUSION

*Lectio divina* is an ancient spiritual art that is being rediscovered in our day. It is a way of allowing the Scriptures to become again what God intended that they should be—a means of uniting us to Himself. In *lectio divina* we discover our own underlying spiritual rhythm. We experience God in a gentle oscillation back and forth between spiritual activity and receptivity, in the movement from practice into contemplation and back again into spiritual practice.

*Lectio divina* teaches us about the God who truly loves us. In *lectio divina* we dare to believe that our loving Father continues to extend His embrace to us today. And His embrace is real. In His word we experience ourselves as personally loved by God—as the recipients of a word which He gives uniquely to each of us whenever we turn to Him in the Scriptures.

Finally, *lectio divina* teaches us about ourselves. In *lectio divina* we discover that there is no place in our hearts, no interior corner or closet that cannot be opened and offered to God. God teaches us in *lectio divina* what it means to be members of His royal priesthood—a people called to consecrate all of our memories, our hopes and our dreams to Christ.

# TWO APPROACHES to GROUP *LECTIO DIVINA*

## 1. *Lectio Divina* Shared in Community

### (A) Listening for the Gentle Touch of Christ the Word
*(The Literal Sense)*

1. One person reads aloud (twice) the passage of scripture, as others are attentive to some segment that is especially meaningful to them.

2. **Silence** for 1-2 minutes. Each hears and silently repeats a word or phrase that attracts.

3. Sharing aloud: (A word or phrase that has attracted each person.) A simple statement of one or a few words. **No elaboration.**

### (B) How Christ the Word speaks to ME
*(The Allegorical Sense)*

4. Second reading of same passage by another person.
5. **Silence** for 2-3 minutes. Reflect on "Where does the content of this reading touch my life today?"
6. Sharing aloud: **Briefly:** "I hear, I see..."

### (C) What Christ the Word Invites me to DO
*(The Moral Sense)*

7. Third reading by still another person.
8. **Silence** for 2-3 minutes. Reflect on "I believe that God wants me to . . . . . . today/this week."

9. Sharing aloud: at somewhat greater length the results of each one's reflection. (Be especially aware of what is shared by the person to your right.)

10. After full sharing, pray for the person to your right.

   **Note:** Anyone may "pass" at any time. If instead of sharing with the group you prefer to pray silently, simply state this aloud and conclude your silent prayer with *Amen.*

## 2. *Lectio* on Life: Applying *Lectio Divina* to my personal Salvation History

*Purpose:* to apply a method of prayerful reflection to a life/work incident (instead of to a scripture passage)

### A. Listening for the Gentle Touch of Christ the Word *(The Literal Sense)*

1. Each person quiets the body and mind: relax, sit comfortably but alert, close eyes, attune to breathing . . .
2. Each person gently reviews events, situations, sights, encounters that have happened since the beginning of the retreat/or during the last month at work.

### B. Gently Ruminating, Reflecting *(Meditatio—Meditation)*

3. Each person allows the self to focus on one such offering.

   a) Recollect the setting, sensory details, sequence of events, etc.

   b) Notice where the greatest energy seemed to be evoked. Was there a turning point or shift?

   c) In what ways did God seem to be present? To what extent was I aware then? Now?

### C. Prayerful Consecration, Blessing *(Oratio—Prayer)*

4. Use a word or phrase from the Scriptures to inwardly consecrate—to offer up to God in prayer—the incident and interior reflections. Allow God to accept and bless them as your gift.

### D. Accepting Christ's Embrace; Silent Presence to the Lord *(Contemplatio—Contemplation)*

5. Remain in silence for some period.

### E. Sharing Our *Lectio* Experience with Each Other *(Operatio—Action; works)*

6. Leader calls the group back into "community."
7. All share briefly (or remain in continuing silence).

# THE SCHOOL OF THE WORD

## CARLO MARIA CARDINAL MARTINI

IT can hardly be denied, I think, that the western world is today experiencing a severe crisis of spiritual desolation. It no longer perceives the mystery of God as present in its major institutions and in the symbols that permeate its public life.

This interior aridity threatens everyone; in particular, it stifles Christians, who are unable to give expression in their daily lives to their faith in the living God. Beyond question, therefore, the Church must help the baptized to make the transition from a traditional faith based on habit and derived from the environment to a personal, interior faith based on conviction and capable of resisting the onslaught of secularism and atheism.

This kind of faith, understood as a dynamic process, is fed and deepened by hearing the word of God. From the very beginning of my episcopal ministry in Milan, my travels through the diocese made clear to me the need people have of the revealed word, their desire to join others in praying and listening to God's word, and the real feasibility of this kind of joint effort.

I also found a certain ignorance of Scripture among even the most highly educated. I therefore resolved to respond as best I could to the exhortation issued by Vatican II in its Constitution on Divine Revelation: that all of the faithful should have direct access to the Bible, because *contact* with the word of God brings an unsuspected wealth of life that is offered as a gift to every Christian. I myself have been reading the Scriptures for over forty years, and at every reading I am astonished to find them utterly new; at every reading I experience the jolt to mind and feelings that stirs a sense of human values and puts me in touch with the values of God.

I was convinced, then, that today, more than in times past, the pages of the Bible can deepen faith by awakening a consciousness of mystery, an openness to the infinite, a movement toward God, and an understanding of God's ways in history. I therefore developed a method that would enable the entire people of God to approach the texts of the Bible step by step.

This method I called the "School of the Word" or "School of Bible-Reading for the Masses." I began to use it with young people whom I invited to the cathedral on the first Thursday of each month. For five years in a row the young came by the thousands, and in ever increasing numbers, even from a distance and even from other dioceses. Their presence proved that the time we spent together (about two hours) in silence, listening to the word, and reflecting on the texts fed them interiorly.

This past year I suggested that these young people give what they have learned to other young people by setting up other "Schools of the Word" in various parts of the diocese. I then invited adults to the cathedral, and in particular laymen and laywomen who are involved in the life of the parish. Once again, the response was surprisingly good. I have also attempted during days of spiritual retreat, to teach children to select some passages from the Old and New Testaments and to understand them.

The "School of the Word" has gradually become a privileged tool of my pastoral activity and of my desire to foster, in communal form as it were, a holiness that is truly popular and not limited to an elite—a holiness that ignores class barriers, is developed in the most unexpected settings, and has the power to overcome all worldliness and fear.

What is a "School of the Word"? It is a step-by-step approach to the biblical text according to the ancient method of the Fathers, which in turn recalls the method of the rabbis and is known as *lectio divina* ("the reading of God's word").

In the Hebrew world the Scriptures were taught in the schools in a very simple way that was adapted to the people. At the same time, certain basic pedagogical and philological principles were operative, as well as a careful progression; if these principles and this progression were neglected, the teaching became fruitless and even counterproductive.

Here, briefly, are the *principles* and *method* of the pedagogy at work in *lectio divina*:

a) The *principles* governing the approach of the Christian people to the sacred text are four in number:

FIRST, *the unity of the Scriptures.* In a "School of the Word" the students must be made to realize that while the Bible is made up of many books it nonetheless forms a unity, inasmuch as every page speaks of God's great plan for the salvation of the human race. Everything refers to the paschal mystery. It is the effort to relate the various texts of the Bible to the unifying mystery that makes all of them yield a meaning, even those that at first glance have little to do with this mystery.

SECOND, *the humanness* or *"existential relevance" of the Scriptures.* The Scriptures speak to human beings; they give expression to the deepest treasures of the human heart, to the restlessness, sufferings, aspirations, desires, and fears that all human beings share. Individuals find themselves in the Bible, for it puts into words what is permanently human; it lends a voice to the human beings of every age as they speak of their hopes and their distresses. Through simple examples the people learn that the reading of Scripture helps them to that understanding of themselves as individuals and as a community, without which they cannot grasp their own unity or their true relationship to others.

THIRD, *the dynamic character of values.* The Bible expresses values that even today are still developing toward the future of humanity. From the viewpoint of the dynamic movement both of morality and of doctrine the Bible contains values that spur us to advance beyond ourselves by giving us a sense that we human beings are people on a journey. The Bible interacts with human life in a constant movement from life to the word of God and from the word of God back to life.

FOURTH, *the Scriptures are a real presence of Jesus.* A "School of the Word" must help people realize that when they read the Scriptures they can enter into a real communion with Jesus. The expression "real communion" may startle because it echoes the language applied to the eucharistic presence, but Vatican II does not hesitate to assert that the risen Christ is present in the Scriptures and that when we read them or listen to them we can experience this presence.

b) The *method* which Christian tradition has developed for *lectio divina* has four steps: reading, meditation, prayer, contemplation. The sequence is the result of theological and anthropological reflection on the way in which believers approach the word of God in order to assimilate it and make it bear fruit in experience and action.

FIRST, *reading.* The people learn to read and reread a passage by underlining and giving prominence to its key elements: the actions, verbs, acting subjects, attitudes and thoughts, settings, motives for acting. A careful study of all these produces a new and surprising understanding of the text because of the many points that are thus brought to light.

SECOND, *meditation.* In this second phase the people reflect on the abiding value of the passage, by trying to pinpoint the central value in it and its specific message in relation to history and context and situation. The students, whose aim is to discover their authentic selves and find God, single out the attitudes that emerge from the passage on which they are meditating: joy, fear, hope, desire, expectation, and so on.

THIRD, *prayer.* The students are gradually drawn to share the deeper religious sentiments that the text produces or suggests in the name of God; the values assimilated in meditation become motives for praise, thanksgiving, intercession, petition, forgiveness, and so on.

FOURTH, *contemplation.* At some point the multiplicity of sentiments, reflections, and prayers are reduced to unity in contemplation of the mystery of Jesus, the Son of God, a mystery that is contained in every page. This is especially true of the Gospels but it is also true in varying degrees of every passage in the Bible.

The aim, then, of the "School of the Word" is to try to read the word of God in such a way that it turns into prayer in us and sheds light on our lives. It is not possible, of course, to reach this goal in a single leap.

In order to stimulate the people to a prayerful listening to God's word, I usually read and reread a passage aloud, then suggest points for meditation, and, after this, remain silent for awhile. I then continue by praying on the passage I have read, thereby leading into a very simple form of personal contemplation.

It is most important for the people to see that the reading of God's word should make Christians challenge themselves: In what way are my life, my activity, my apostolate becoming a word of God in the light of the definitive Word that is Jesus Christ, present in the Scriptures? When they do this, the "School of the Word," which aims at bringing faith to bear on daily life, will express its radical power in certain interconnected attitudes. These are:

a) *Discernment*, that is, the ability Christians develop, with the grace of the Holy Spirit, to see in their lives what is or is not in conformity with the Gospel. It is a discernment of what is best, at a given moment in history, for themselves, for others, for the Church.

b) *Decision*, or the choice of what is in conformity with the Gospel in their lives.

c) *Action* which follows upon discernment and decision. Only the kind of Christian acting, doing, and thinking that is guided by the Holy Spirit can truly be called spiritual activity "according to God."

With the help of the "School of the Word," Christians will gradually become capable of recognizing, despite the ambiguities of history, the signs and glorious presence of the risen Lord in the midst of His people and the local community. My own experience with the "School of the Word" convinces me that it is a tool to be used by ordinary people, by any of the faithful who desire to live authentically Christian lives in a secularized world.

Life in this secularized world demands people who are contemplative, alert, critical, and courageous; it demands that from time to time they make new choices of a kind not made before; it demands attentiveness and new emphases to which they can be alerted by listening to God's word and being sensitive to the mysterious action of the Holy Spirit in hearts and in history.

Cardinal Martini, archbishop of Milan, gave conferences to the American bishops gathered at Collegeville, Minnesota in June 1986. The translation of his article was prepared by Matthew J. O'Connell and reproduced in the May 1987 issue (Vol. 61, 5) of *Worship* and is reproduced here with the permission of the publishers.

# St. Joseph Bibles and Missals

No. 612/97—Family Bible—White Padded Leather

No. 609/13—Deluxe Leather Bible—Brown, White or Red

No. 825/23—Daily and Sunday Missal—3-Volume Set

# Liturgy of the Hours

No. 409/10—Set of 4 volumes—Flexible Binding

No. 409/13—Set of 4 volumes—Leather Binding

No. 709/13—Set of 4 volumes—Large-print, Leather binding

No. 406/10—*Christian Prayer*—Flexible maroon binding

No. 406/23—*Christian Prayer*—Zipper binding

No. 408/10—*Shorter Christian Prayer*—Flexible binding

No. 415/04—*A Companion to the Liturgy of the Hours: Morning and Evening Prayer*

No. 416/04—*The Divine Office for Dodos: A Step-by-Step Guide to Praying the Liturgy of the Hours*—By Madeline Pecora Nugent

No. 426/04—*Practical Guide to the Liturgy of the Hours*—By Shirley Sullivan

For free catalog contact
www.catholicbookpublishing.com